FOLLOW THE

LEADER

PRAISE FOR *FOLLOW THE LEADER*

Fresh, authentic and applicable – that is how Emmanuel Gobillot approaches the topic of leadership. At last a book about leadership that elevates the conversation beyond the egocentricity of the leader himself. Why do people follow? What an insightful and powerful question to ask. This is one of the only books I have ever read that applies a leadership skill to the business of writing leadership books – it walks a mile in the follower's shoes. As the saying goes, if you have no followers, you are simply out for a walk.
Peter Sheahan, Global bestselling author of *Generation Y, Fl!p* and *Making it Happen*

EMMANUEL GOBILLOT

FOLLOW THE

THE ONE THING GREAT LEADERS HAVE THAT GREAT FOLLOWERS WANT

LEADER

KoganPage

First published in Great Britain and the United States in 2013 by Kogan Page Limited

120 Pentonville Road
London N1 9JN
United Kingdom
www.koganpage.com

1518 Walnut Street, Suite 1100
Philadelphia PA 19102
USA

4737/23 Ansari Road
Daryaganj
New Delhi 110002
India

© Emmanuel Gobillot, 2013

The right of Emmanuel Gobillot to be identified as the author of this work has been asserted by him in accordance with the Copyright, Designs and Patents Act 1988.

ISBN   978 0 7494 6905 4
E-ISBN   978 0 7494 6906 1

British Library Cataloguing-in-Publication Data

A CIP record for this book is available from the British Library.

Library of Congress Cataloging-in-Publication Data

Gobillot, Emmanuel.
  Follow the leader : discover the one thing great leaders have that great followers want / Emmanuel Gobillot.
      pages cm
    ISBN 978-0-7494-6905-4 – ISBN (invalid) 978-0-7494-6906-1   1. Leadership.   2. Ability.
3. Character.   I. Title.
    HM1261.G6315 2013
    303.3′4–dc23
                                                                                    2012041103

Typeset by Graphicraft Limited, Hong Kong
Printed and bound in India by Replika Press Pvt Ltd

A maman, pour m'avoir tout donné

CONTENTS

01 Why do we follow? 11

If we understand why we follow then we start to understand what value leaders provide. It's easy to see the attraction of being a leader, but why would anyone want to follow? Why are we so desperate to give up our ability to choose our own course of action? Find out why we are willing to die for a suit, literally!

02 Emotional logic: the follower's decision-making engine 25

By understanding the mechanics of how followers choose their leaders we can work to meet their demands. But are their choices always rational? How can we tackle something that isn't? And what does the phrase 'the duck is ready to eat' have to do with any of this?

03 Charisma: the one thing that matters 41

Ask any follower why they admire a particular leader and chances are charisma will be the answer. Yet few people know how to define it, never mind develop it. The good news is that once you understand emotional logic charisma becomes clear. We can learn a lot about it from the Mona Lisa. She knows something we don't and that's why she has that knowing smile.

*stuffed toys, I want to show you how to build and retain integrity.
I will show you how integrity is a process of alignment and what to
do when that alignment is broken.*

09   Simplicity   139

*Given that followers make their decision to follow incredibly quickly,
we must be able to give them as much of the data they require in
a format that is as simple as possible. How do you build simplicity
without becoming simplistic? What are the components of simplicity
and the tools used to build it? I will use a key rule of business books
to find the answers.*

PART FOUR   The achievement dimension   153

10   Measurement   155

*Leadership is not given – it is lent. For leadership to be sustained,
followers must have a way to know that progress towards a vision
is being made. For this they need markers. Measures are those
markers. But how do you create measures that are bought into?
How do you know which measures truly matter? In this chapter
we meet a British scientist and a French engineer who can help
us with that.*

11   Action   171

*As a leader you must reassure followers that you are capable of
delivering on your promises. It is your actions that provide that
reassurance. But are all actions the same? How can we differentiate
the actions that take us forward from those that can hold us back?
Let me introduce you to the tallest leader I know.*

Concluding thoughts   187

LIST OF FIGURES

ACKNOWLEDGEMENTS

There is a complete symbiotic relationship between my consulting, speaking and writing work. My consulting practice fuels my research, which dictates my writing, which in turn provides me with the chance to speak, which lets me meet new clients for my consulting practice. This may be a neat business model but it is a nightmare when it comes to the business of acknowledgements. How do I thank the thousands of people who I speak to every year? How can I determine who has influenced what? Anyway, at this point, I have had to make a choice and making that choice also means I need to make an apology. So to all those who have influenced me through the conversations we have had or ideas we exchanged and, in some cases, whose names I don't even know, please accept my apologies.

There are however some people who have clearly and pretty much directly influenced this book. Their support, advice and friendship have carried me through the lonely writing experience.

For a number of years now I have worked with the Carlsberg Group on the development of their emerging global leaders. Meeting such enthusiastic, dedicated and fun people is not only a joy but forces me constantly to reassess my views of leadership and development in a global context. Thank you to Jørgen Buhl Rasmussen, Group CEO, and Claudia Schlossberger, SVP Group HR, for giving me that chance. Above all I would like to thank Stefanie Groth, Group Talent Director, who has always found the right questions to ask to prompt me to take my thinking forward, and has been a delight to work for. I am also eternally grateful to her for agreeing never to publish the photos of my Bollywood dancing.

Thanks to Stephen Cunningham, Group Talent Director, and Alison Wilcox, HR Director for Africa, Middle East and Asia Pacific, I have been lucky to have met all of the top 250 executives of Vodafone globally and some of their direct reports too. All of them, in some way, have had an impact on my work. I would like to thank Vittorio Colao, Group CEO, and Ronald Schellekens, Group HR Director, for giving me the chance to embark on The Vodafone Way journey with them. In particular I owe a huge debt of gratitude to Raja Al-Khatib, Chief of Staff to the Group CEO and Group Director of Internal Communications, and Julia Jack, Business Transformation Lead and The Vodafone Way Programme Manager for all their support and challenges. I must also mention Liz Nelson, Alison Clarke and Lou McEwen from the events team for coping with me and my ideas through my work with Vodafone.

If my consulting clients fuel my writing and research, it is my speaking career that helps me test and challenge my ideas. There is nothing more energizing that the hundreds of conversations I have each year with so many diverse audiences. Thank you to all those who have trusted me enough to give me time at their events. In particular I would like to thank Dr Neil Wooding and his team at Public Service Management Wales for inviting me to speak at both their Winter and Summer Schools at just the right times to help me shape this book. Also a big thank you to Martin and Farah Perelmuter and their team at Speaker Spotlight, and Brian Palmer and his team at National Speakers Bureau for being the kind of agents who speakers dream of getting but seldom do.

Finally, when it comes to my writing, I must thank my publishers Kogan Page and, in particular, Liz Gooster whose project this was. Liz's feedback made this a much better book than it otherwise would have been. Liz has demonstrated endless patience as I shared with her my plentiful views about what I believe constitutes good and bad design for books and covers. She has mastered the skill of making an author feel listened to, understood and happy. Thanks for making this a fun project.

There is a very important person I must also thank for all her help. As Group HR Director of MITIE plc, Katherine Thomas has challenged me to make my ideas practical. As an unpaid consultant she has read, reviewed and corrected all of the drafts of this book. And as Katherine, my partner, she has supported and encouraged me through the too-many-to-count times when I thought about giving up, without ever losing her patience. I couldn't have done it without her.

Last but not in any way least I must thank Charlotte and George who, with some grace and a great deal of humour, manage to cope with the self-absorbed and grumpy papa they were unlucky to get. I love you both.

But of course what every author knows is that without someone buying the book publishers would show little interest in publishing it so I would also like to take this opportunity to thank the people who have given me the chance to continue writing by purchasing my previous books. As they will know, I always apply the same disclaimer at the end of my acknowledgements. So here goes. Any omissions or mistakes are entirely mine. I just thank the people named above for helping me keep them to a minimum.

INTRODUCTION
THE WRONG QUESTION

Let's play a thought experiment. Think of a leader you admire. It can be any leader, from any field. The only restriction is that the leader has to be real. Whilst fictional leaders are not allowed, dead ones are. You don't even have to narrow it down to one; you can choose a few.

If you are like the hundreds of global executives to whom I have posed this question, your chosen leaders will be from the fields of politics (eg Mahatma Gandhi, Nelson Mandela, Margaret Thatcher, Francois Mitterrand and Barack Obama), the military (eg Generals Patton and Schwarzkopf) or both (eg Dwight D Eisenhower, General De Gaulle or Winston Churchill) as well as religious and civil society (eg Reverends Martin Luther King, Jr, and Jesse Jackson, Mother Teresa or Lech Walesa). They may well also be drawn from a long list of managers of a variety of national sports (from American Football's Vince Lombardi to English Football's Alex Ferguson). If, unlike many of the executives I have asked, you opted for business leaders, chances are the names will be from the A list (eg Welch, Branson, Gates and Jobs). But, on the basis of what I have experienced previously, I'm willing to place a strong bet that it is highly unlikely that you chose your immediate boss. But that's not the point – at least not yet.

In fact I don't even mind if you are completely different from the rest of my sample. The point of asking you to think of a leader you admire is to take you to the next stage of the experiment. That stage is to answer the fundamental question that is on most people's mind when they think about leadership. This question is: 'What do great leaders do?' It is a powerful question the answer to which has generated hundreds of leadership books with thousands of 'success to-do lists'. So here is Part Two of our thought experiment. Thinking about the leaders you identified (or for that matter any of the ones I mentioned above), can you identify the attributes that made them great?

You and I have met enough successful executives in our careers to know that they come in all shape and sizes. So to look for elements shared by all the leaders you have chosen is an interesting but also a difficult exercise. Some are extroverts whilst others are introverts. Some are loud and others quiet. Some speak whilst others listen. Some think fast whilst others reflect slowly. Some act whilst others delegate. Defining what is common often leads to a conclusion about what is average. Given the leadership development market is valued at $65bn, average just doesn't seem like an appropriate starting point.

There is however something all of these admired leaders have in common. That one thing is also what truly differentiates the great from the average. Yet it is also the one that is often ignored by leadership books. It seldom features in leadership articles other than as an output or an afterthought. That one thing is typically treated as a by-product of great leadership rather than its foundation. You should be offended as well as concerned about this, for that one thing is you.

What is special about the leader or leaders you thought of, and is true of all great leaders, is that they are chosen by one or more people as the person from whom they wish to take direction. It is followers who make leaders. Yet, in our thirst for answers to the question 'What do great leaders do?' we seldom stop to consider a far more interesting question that drives the very essence of leadership effectiveness; 'What do great followers want?'[1]

Given that most leadership books are written for business people and that in most organizations it is other leaders, rather than followers, who choose leaders, this oversight might not seem altogether too big a deal. But even if followers do not choose their leaders, it is their efforts and willingness to follow that will determine how effective these leaders will be.

Over the last couple of years I have been researching the 'What do followers want?' question. The idea for my interest is a simple but a powerful one. If we understand what great followers want, we no longer need to worry about what great leaders do. We no longer need to aspire to become poor copies of other leaders. Aping others was always a flawed strategy anyway. Given that our behaviour is a function of who we are and the situation we find ourselves in and that none of us are either the leaders we admire nor, thankfully in many cases, in the situations in which they succeeded, this tactic was always doomed to fail.

But all of us can be the leaders our followers want. We can learn to become the best possible version of ourselves, with our own style and our own characteristics. No longer will we need to try to develop the average in our search for differentiation. We can get back to being our unique selves, only this time a better version of these – one that appeals to the great followers we want.

Throughout the course of my research a structure for this book emerged that follows the story I encountered. The narrative is best summarized as a series of questions.

Why do we follow?

If we start by understanding our need for leaders we will have a better idea of how to gauge great leadership. It turns out that we all look for leadership for the same reasons. Some are pretty straightforward and obvious, others more surprising. In Chapter 1 I will look at these reasons and what they can teach us. What we will discover is that our need for leaders provides us with the clues as to what constitutes great leadership. The temptation at this stage would be to jump to working out how we provide what followers want. However there is a critical step before that. Whilst we know what followers look for, we are yet to work out how they go about finding it. That decision-making process lies at the heart of great leadership. So in Chapter 2, I will move on to the second critical question.

How do we choose the people we follow?

By developing a full picture of followers' decision-making processes, we can start to reveal the strategies we may need to attract them to our cause. What we will discover in Chapter 2 is what I call the 'emotional logic' of decision making. The fact that we are not rational beings affects the decisions we make when we choose our leaders. This is why I opted for the term 'emotional logic' to describe that process. It implies both a visceral and an analytical aspect. It is neither entirely conscious nor unconscious, nor is it purely emotional or logical, but it can be identified and explained by identifying the three dimensions all followers' brains focus on. I will call them the 'values dimension', the 'character dimension' and the 'achievement dimension'.

As we will see, emotional logic is the key that opens the door to the one thing we all look for – charisma. Although it is the first attribute most people use to describe what they are looking for in leaders, leadership development experts tend not to like the idea of charisma. It is not only hard to define but it also implies an inbred quality that is impossible to develop.

In Chapter 3 I break down what followers mean by charisma and show how this underpins emotional logic. There are eight elements that make up charisma. Underpinning the values dimension of emotional logic are Compassion and Hope. Asperity, Rhetoric, Integrity and Simplicity are the elements that make up the character dimension. Finally Measurements and Action underpin the achievement dimension of emotional logic. These elements not only spell out what charisma means (literally) but they also offer us the elements that we need to develop to become the leaders others want to follow.

The good news is that by working out what charisma means to followers we realize that each and every one of us can develop the skills necessary to display it. Yes charisma is indeed a gift as its Greek etymology suggests, but it is not a gift from the gods; rather it is one offered by followers to those prepared to work through its constituent parts. Followers decide how you answer their emotional logic dimensions. They decide whether you pass the values, character and achievement tests. How you approach each dimension and what you do to fulfil it are all determinants of the charisma followers will allocate to you and, as a result, your success in attracting them to your cause. The remainder of the book is therefore devoted to helping you meet the challenge offered by the next question.

How do we provide what followers are looking for?

I made the point that we are at our best when we are ourselves, but leadership is a complex system. Everything we aim for, we do and we are, interacts with the situations we find ourselves in to produce the outcomes others experience. So whilst a book is by its very nature sequential, emotional logic isn't. I have therefore tried to ensure that the narrative links the chapters together, whilst at the same time enabling the ideas to be read in whatever order you choose. The key to success is to meet all the requirements of emotional logic, not the order in which you tackle your development.

The aim of every aspiring leader should be to move people emotionally in a way that releases their discretionary effort in the act of followership. People who follow blindly and obey are of little use to the modern corporate leader – hence my choice of the term 'charisma' to describe the type of leadership I uncovered in my research.

When we force or coerce others into doing anything using positional power alone (albeit well intentioned and articulated), we are pushing them to do something. We do not so much lead them as push them into a submissive stance (you cannot push from the front!).

Pushing others can be effective, if what we are looking to get done is limited, well defined and time-bound. Yet, today's workplace is characterized by the need for problem solving and solution searching, neither of which can be described as linear, simple, repetitive occupations. A leader cannot coerce someone into effective problem solving. We can demand the action but will seldom get the solution.

Today's work requires initiative. When we are looking for people to take initiative, to define the possible whilst aiming for the impossible, we can no longer afford to push them; we have to provide genuine leadership to them. We need them to come to us and invest their own energy. We need to pull rather than push. We need to make the environment sufficiently attractive to make them want to provide not only effort but discretionary effort, in the same way as we aim to get customers to release their discretionary spend on the products of our work.

The difference between these two push and pull strategies is analogous to the difference between charisma that acts as a magnet and control that acts as a cattle prod. Both get others to move and both are activated by leaders. But where the positional leader secures the physical engagement of others, the charismatic leader earns the emotional engagement of followers. It is in that emotional engagement that real value lies.

In many ways we get the followers we deserve. Every fully functioning human being is motivated. We all have motives that drive us towards particular actions. To describe direct reports as not being motivated is simply to describe people who have stopped following. My premise in this book is that if they have stopped following it is due to the leader losing their appeal not to followers losing the will to follow. By developing a field of attraction through the activation of the three emotional-logic dimensions, charismatic leaders are assured of being surrounded by the talent they need.

By its very nature, charisma attracts people who are made of 'the right stuff', have the 'right kind of energy' and are willing to commit that energy (actual and discretionary) to the cause at hand. But of course, charismatic leaders, like magnets, can repel as many people as they attract. Whilst in our inclusive times this can be seen as a negative, I will suggest, in endeavouring to redefine charisma, that it is a positive. Without rejection, there can be no choice, and without choice there can be no commitment. Far from being a flaw, the fact that charisma polarizes people is one of its critical strengths.

What drove me to write this book now is that even a casual glance at the news reminds us of the need for a renewed focus on leadership. From uprisings to economic crises, people are looking for leaders to transform their landscape. Today leadership that gets results happens without titles and across lines. It coincides with a refusal to accept the status quo and requires the ability to work in uncertainty by embracing massive change as a massive opportunity. As we get to understand the interaction between followership and leadership, developing a full understanding of charisma becomes critical as it will help us build the one thing great leaders have that great followers want. So from Chapter 4 to Chapter 11 I will analyse and explain each of the elements that make up charisma in turn, and provide strategies and practical steps for its development.

Finally I will conclude the book by offering you some of the principles I have come to value in my practice to enable you to get the maximum value out of any efforts to develop the ideas contained in this book.

As I close this introduction, let me say a few words about how this book is organized. In my first book, *The Connected Leader*, I introduced a couple of devices readers and reviewers seemed to like. The first was a quick overview at the beginning of each chapter of the questions that chapter sought to answer. I followed this at the end of each chapter with a quick 30-second recap. The idea was to enable you to dip in and out of the book whilst retaining the thread. In my second book, *Leadershift*, I dropped the questions at the beginning, only keeping the recap at the end.

A number of readers were kind enough to give me feedback that they liked the opening questions so I have reintroduced them here. Over the last year I have become acutely aware that I am spending much more time on Twitter than I spend writing and reading blog entries. I like the idea of being able to get to the essence of a message in 140 characters, which leaves me free to then explore the idea further through any link attached. For this reason I have changed 'the 30-second recap' to 'the tweet' where I have endeavoured to capture the essence of a chapter in 140 characters or less (leaving you free to explore the chapter in more detail if you feel the need).

But enough of the outline – let's get on with the story.

Note

1 Many will point out that what great followers want is not always the same as what they need. Despite a certain implied arrogance there is often some truth in that statement, yet, if we work on the premise that leaders earned that title by the very fact that people chose to follow them, the distinction becomes pretty irrelevant. If you want to give followers what they need you will have to give it to them in a way that they want.

PART ONE
EMOTIONAL LOGIC

Whilst in today's organizations we have come to believe that the role makes the leader, this has never been further from the truth. Being given a 'leadership role' does not create a leader. It is followers who make leaders. Having that role may result in followers who have been allocated through some reporting line (straight, dotted or otherwise), but it does not generate followers who have chosen to be led. It certainly does not create followers who have elected to replace their self-determination with the belief that they will be better served under the stewardship of an individual.

So if followers make leaders, then the natural place to start on our journey to discover great leadership is to understand the reasons why, and the basis on which, followership decisions are made. This is what we will explore in this first part.

CHAPTER 1
WHY DO WE FOLLOW?

Underpinning question and why it matters

Why do we follow?

Trying to become a better leader by studying the characteristics of great leaders is futile. It is followers (through their choices and hard work) who decide who leads and how great the leader will be. Successful development strategies start with one key question: why do followers choose to follow? The answer will enable anyone interested in becoming a better leader to uncover the 'mechanisms of followership' in order to create the attraction strategies necessary for effective leadership.

To everyone watching that bright morning in 1955 the situation was clear. They were in no doubt. The man was crazy. He was risking his life.

Yet, an hour later, so would they.

The man in question was an average-looking man, dressed casually, standing at a traffic light. The strange behaviour witnessed by others was that every time the traffic sign showed 'do not cross', the man would cross. People looked on wondering how long it might be before he would get run over.

An hour later the same man came back. This time, he was dressed in a suit. Incredibly every time he attempted to cross at the wrong time, the crowd followed, seemingly putting their lives at risk for the sake of a suit.

I have written about Lefkowitz, Blake and Mouton's experiment before.[1] I have always found it a fascinating example of our bias for 'followership'. What these three researchers did when they set up their catchily entitled experiment – 'status factor in pedestrian violation of traffic signals' – was to highlight two fundamental paradigms of leadership. The first is our innate desire to follow. The second is that this desire leads us to making choices about what or who to follow.

These paradigms raise the key questions anyone interested in being a leader, developing their leadership skills, or indeed developing other leaders, should have in mind. Why do we follow? How do we decide who to follow?

Too often we start the journey towards becoming a better/great leader the wrong way round. We focus on other leaders in the hope of identifying killer characteristics that we hope to ape. At other times we focus on ourselves to understand why we do what we do, with a view to managing our impact better. These are not worthless pursuits (there is nothing wrong with watching what the best do, or with seeking self-awareness) but they are purely academic until someone decides to follow us. That act alone is the only one that will make us a leader.

So whilst few do so, I would argue that our time is better spent at the start of our journey by understanding the reasons people follow. Without followers there can be no leadership. Understanding their needs and choices will help us understand the mechanisms leading to their fulfilment. So let's start our journey at the beginning and try to answer the question:

Why do we follow?

The beginning of an answer can be found in Africa. It's not hard to see why tourists would want to join birds in flocking to South Africa's east coast. Following the southern garden route from the tip of the great continent upwards leads you through a breathtakingly beautiful and lush landscape reminiscent of 19th-century pictures of paradise. But it's not just birds and humans that are keen on the place. Each year, starting in June, sardine shoals, tens of metres deep and several miles long, make their shimmering way along the KwaZulu Natal coast.

The giant sardine shoal is a wonder for some and a meal for others. Attracted by the plentiful bounty, in some cases from several miles away, tens of thousands of dolphins and birds, and thousands of sharks follow the shoal.

To witness the event is to witness nature's amazing circle of life, with dolphins even timing their breeding seasons to coincide with the availability of sardines on which their young depend for survival. Like cowboys rounding up their herds, they gather up the sardines in what are referred to as 'bait balls'.

The threatened sardines, surrounded not only by dolphins at their sides but also by sharks underneath and birds above, instinctively group together as a defence mechanism (an individual fish is at a much lower risk of being eaten if it is part of a large group). The ensuing feeding frenzy is as spectacularly deadly as it is wonderfully choreographed. The surrounded sardine ball has no chance. Dolphins swim into the ball from the sides whilst sharks come up from underneath and birds launch aerial assaults on their prey.

Sardines move in and out from the centre of the shoals and ball baits to their extremities and back again at regular intervals to minimize the chances of being eaten. Their amazing numbers ensure that, despite the countless attacks, the shoal size remains pretty much the same to the untrained eye.

There are obvious advantages to being a follower. From sardines and termites to monkeys and sheep via birds and bees, nature is full of examples of herd behaviour. The prime concern of life being to survive, the safety afforded by following others is obvious. And in that we humans are not much different from other species; we too have evolved a followership instinct.

Standing in front of Christ's College in Cambridge, England, watching the busy shoppers hurrying along on St Andrews Street is reminiscent of that herd instinct. What is less obvious is that, it is in the college rooms behind the walls, that a key contribution to explaining that instinct was made.

It was in these rooms, in 1828, that a young Darwin, sent to Cambridge by his father as a punishment for not studying medicine hard enough at Edinburgh, developed a passion that would leave an indelible mark on the world. In his *On the Origins of Species*, Darwin set out his theory of natural selection. Individuals who adapt better to their environment – the fittest, not the strongest as is often postulated – are more successful at reproducing. As their genes are passed on, species develop and continue to adapt.

Back in humankind's most primitive times, before we ever thought of agriculture, even less organizations, for our nomadic forebears, as for sardines, following facilitated both their survival and ability to adapt. By coming together in groups our ancestors sought safety. Faced with a charging mammoth, hunting alone would have been stupid, and stupidity in those times was typically rewarded by death. The ones who could adapt to following survived more often than the lone hunters and gatherers and as a result passed on their 'followership genes' down through generations.

Whilst following the group for survival makes sense of followership, it does not, in and of itself, create the need for a leader. There are plenty of examples of successfully evolved leaderless, self-coordinating groups in nature. So, apart from the obvious – human beings are not sardines, even though anyone witnessing crowded rush hour trains in any city in the world might disagree – why do we follow leaders as well as the herd?

Our activities have always been varied and social. It is not hard to imagine that from an evolutionary standpoint some of our ancestors were better equipped to undertake some tasks than others. It is these varied activities and abilities that created leadership. Whilst hunting in a group makes better sense than hunting alone, for the group to follow the best hunter makes even more sense. In fighting, it made sense to follow the strongest warrior. The same argument stands for most social activities. Primeval leadership was distributed leadership: in other words, it flowed through the group, depending on the task at hand.

As these tasks evolved and our social lives became richer in their complexity, the need for single-point leadership, in the form of an individual, became more prominent. In trying to resolve complex social issues, it made sense to defer to a group of wise elders. And as led groups were more successful than leaderless ones, nature selected the 'leadership' genes to go hand in hand with the 'followership' ones.

The advantages for leaders were obvious: the status afforded by leadership gave more opportunities for reproduction. For the followers the act of following was reinforced not only by the safety it afforded but also by the opportunity to learn at the feet of the leaders and the accompanying hope of one day becoming a leader. And so our fixation with leadership began. This in some way starts to help us answer the second question at the outset of this chapter:

How do we decide who to follow?

If there are clear evolutionary benefits to the acts of leading and following it would also appear that there are dangers attached in following, depending on who we choose to follow. After all by following, you relinquish your individual freedom, trusting that others will help you achieve your personal goals. That trust might not always be repaid, depending on the choices you make.

The way people followed the suited man in our earlier example does seem to indicate that, rationally speaking, not all leaders are worth following. In the same way as following ideas and fads can be dangerous, so too is following people. From tulips to dot coms, the consequences of following the latest 'safe bet' can be disastrous. So how exactly do we make the choice of who or what to follow?

As a Frenchman, I was brought up to believe the ultimate statement of enlightenment bequeathed to us by Descartes 'je pense donc je suis' ('I think therefore I am'). Later, at university, as I studied philosophy of the mind along with logic and metaphysics, it seemed that the answer to the question 'how do we decide who to follow' was clearly best grounded in the rational, ana-lytical, cool-headed, and therefore fully conscious, weighing up of alternatives based on some utilitarian model of what's best for me and, at the same time, causes minimum harm to others.

We can deconstruct the suit experiment following that rational model. The reasoning goes something like this. As followers, we look for attributes that make us trust someone will provide a benefit to us (eg crossing a road quicker). The man in a suit is probably a business man and therefore (at least back then) someone we perceive to be a trustworthy member of our community (ie some-one with our best interests at heart and a proven ability to guide us). That being the case, following a man in a suit makes sense.

After all, even if arguably things have changed since the 50s, we can all relate to these findings. That's pretty much the reasoning we go through every time someone knocks on our door. We have a quick glance through the window to see who it might be and provided they look and act the part (whatever that part is in your culture and background), we feel safe to open the door.

The suit experiment and other similar examples only go to prove what is common knowledge – we follow because we are attracted to attributes (be they physical, intellectual or moral) we see in others. The reason this matters to us here is that if we understand the attributes (eg a suit) and develop them (eg wear it) we will attract others. If you want to be followed, follow the recipe. The funny thing, though, is that it always takes time for knowledge to become common and as a result common knowledge tends to lag behind actual knowledge. And so it is here.

In our quest for simple recipes we miss the two critical points raised by the experiment. The first is that decisions are not made solely on a rational basis. The people standing at the light did not go through a conscious reasoning process before they followed the suit. They just followed. If we were to ask them why they followed, the closest we will get to a truthful reason (rather than a post-event rationalization) is 'because it felt like the right thing to do'; 'It kind of made sense'.

There is a reason we call this kind of reasoning a gut feeling – it doesn't go anywhere near our rational brain and, strangely or interestingly, we tend to associate feelings with parts of the body other than the head (heart or gut). In fact we even go so far as to say, 'I've lost my head' when overtaken by strong emotions. Crimes of passion carry lesser sentences (in France at least) on the basis that feelings and cognition (and therefore intent) are disconnected!

As well as being 'non-rational', the second aspect of decision making highlighted by the suit experiment is the unconscious nature of rapid decision making. Few if any of us consciously stop and analyse a situation before crossing a road. Can you imagine in a crowded street if you stopped to analyze the flow of traffic and everyone else did so before proceeding? The street would quickly look like one of those viral flash mob performances when everyone stops for a given time in a train station.

Our brain makes thousands of decisions on our unconscious behalf that we consciously rationalize later. The reason we find it hard to go beyond 'it felt right' as an explanation for our decision is that we are not fully aware of our own choices. The brain is a funny thing. It has no pain receptors so we can never be physically aware of its functioning, however much concentration we try to devote to the task.

So to make progress on our journey of understanding what followers look for in their leaders we can't rely solely on asking them. We will have to investigate the two sides of the decision-making coin to work out if it is simply tossed or if something more complex and carefully reasoned takes place. If it is the former and there is no actual way of knowing how people make followership choices, then this will be a short book. If it is the latter and we can understand what drives our choices, then we can work out how to influence them, or more appropriately how to become the preferred choice of others.

Understanding how people make decisions will therefore require us to investigate two aspects of how we go about deciding. The first is the rational versus emotional side (ie do we think therefore we are, or do we feel therefore we do?). The second is the conscious versus unconscious side (ie do we actually always know why we do what we do?).

In my experience there are really only two safe answers when faced with either/or propositions. One is 'it depends' and the other is 'both'! And so it is with the two we face here. To say that the brain has two distinct circuits that work in isolation from each other is an appealing way to simplify. It allows us to think we can safely focus on reason without having to worry about emotions, or the other way around. However it is worth remembering that the brain is not a collection of isolated circuits, each responsible for its own bit of behaviour. Circuits act, react and interact in unison.

There are two regions of the brain that we must look at when we try to understand the interplay between the rational and the emotional. These sit in the prefrontal cortex, the area of the brain towards the front of the head, which is associated with cognition, decision making and our social behaviour. The first is the dorsolateral prefrontal cortex (DLPFC). Whilst not exclusively responsible for these functions (as mentioned above it would be oversimplifying to isolate areas of the brain for particular functions), the DLPFC is critical in integrating sensory information with the regulation of intellectual function and resulting action. In other words, this part of our brain is where conscious choice resides. It is where we hold our working memory, weigh evidence and make conscious choices.

The other area of interest is the ventromedial prefrontal cortex (VMPFC). Unlike the DLPFC, the VMPFC can be thought of more as the emotional circuitry of decision making. It is critical to emotional regulation through the amygdala, sometimes referred to – in oversimplified shorthand – as part of our reptilian brain. It plays an important role in decision making in uncertainty, where guessing plays a key role, linking the body's feedback with mental models to make emotional associations that help decision making.[2]

To understand how these systems interact in our decision making, let's leave the scientific explanation behind and look at an example. Let's go back to the 1950s of our suited American road-crossing pedestrian, but this time one year later and in France.

For most people going about their daily business, 1956 was like any other year in Paris. Big events were happening in the world, as they always do, but it was small events happening in the homes and cafés of the city that were most likely to mark people's daily lives. And so it was in a bar near the Gare de Lyon when Albert Renaud walked in to buy wine and cigarettes.

Although Albert Renaud was a regular, many wished he'd stay away. He was not only unfriendly, he was frankly rude. A bad-mannered man with a bad-mannered life, he would pass away the evening getting progressively more drunk and progressively more rude. Maybe he was trying to forget some-thing or make up for something else but the only benefit of his being out at the bar was that he was not at home, inflicting violence on his wife. Albert Renaud was the sort of man whose sole purpose seems to be to remind us of the kindness of others.

So when Albert came into the bar that evening and asked for a packet of cigarettes and a bottle of wine without his trademark bad temper, even apologizing for not being able to stay as his sweet wife was asleep in their apartment, regulars wondered what had happened to him.

It was not until 10 days later when Madame Verrier, Albert's mother-in-law, made contact, alarmed at not having heard from her daughter, that the truth would emerge. When she walked into their apartment an unkempt, by now bearded, Albert answered the door, almost pleased to see the mother-in-law he had so despised. The apartment floor was covered with the 10 bottles of wine he had bought daily for the last 10 days and countless half-smoked cigarette butts. From then on, events took a turn from the strange to the newsworthy.

It was just after Albert had told her in the calmest of voices to speak more quietly as her daughter was asleep that the Madame Verrier realized she was indeed lying, inert, on her bed. She was indeed asleep but in that long sleep none of us wake up from, having been shot three times at close range.

To add to the baffling nature of the situation, the police noticed whilst questioning him that Albert too had been shot. In fact he had shot himself in the head shortly after murdering his wife. By some twist of fate the bullet had entered his skull without actually killing him. Yet, the bizarre thing was that, for all intents and purposes, the man speaking to the police bore no resemblance to Albert Renaud. Softly spoken, unable to display the smallest amount of aggression, Albert only stood there wondering what all the commotion was about. His wife was asleep and all he wanted was to be left in peace.

By shooting himself in the head, Albert Renaud did not commit the suicide he had intended. Rather, he had managed unknowingly to conduct a surgical procedure banned in France. Albert Renaud had lobotomized himself. A bullet managed to do what no amount of human kindness had done – fundamentally alter his personality. Albert Renaud 2.0 was a sweet, pleasant man who could not even defend himself in court as defence assumes disagreement and disagreeing was a capacity Albert could no longer master. When any form of aggression deserts you, you can no longer function.

The new Albert would eventually be condemned for a crime the old Albert, absent from the dock, had committed, but then again justice systems, especially in such gruesome circumstances, tend to go for the simplest solution for the sake of expediency.

A big event in a small life doesn't necessarily make for a big event on a global scale and the case of Albert Renaud was quickly forgotten by the world, relegated to the pages of crime books of the type people read to pass the time on holiday beaches.[3] But sometimes, when the right people hear about small events they have major consequences. It seems that in Paris, France, in 1956 no one had heard or cared about Cavendish, New England USA. If they had, they might have seen the parallels between Albert's story and a case that happened roughly 100 years before on the other side of the world, which is now confined to the annals of neurology rather than psychological thrillers. Both stories are, in fact, the mirror image of each other.

It was in 1848 that a hard-working and polite Phineas Gage was working with his gang of men on the railroad. His men loved Phineas almost as much as the bar customers hated Albert. His superiors thought highly of him. Gage lived the kind of life that doesn't make headlines but makes the lives of others worth living. He was not only a kind man, he was a strong leader. At five foot six and in good shape he was the kind of leader who rolls up his sleeves and gets stuck in to progress the work.

On that fateful day, Gage and his team were laying down explosives to make the road flatter for the tracks to be laid on. A split second of inattention is all it took to denude Phineas of what made him himself – his personality. Phineas didn't see the blast coming as he stood over it with a metal rod. The rod flew up from his hand, traversed his head, taking with it some cheek bone and an eye. It came to rest some hundred feet away as Gage landed on his back.

But as Renaud would later do, Gage proved that the unthinkable can happen. By the time he was taken back down to the town of Cavendish he could talk about the accident more reliably than his men, who were still suffering from the shock of having witnessed it. For all intents and purposes Phineas was alive and well. But as Dr Harlow who attended to Gage would later write, Phineas Gage was no longer Phineas Gage.

Unlike Renaud, whose character improved following the shock, Phineas's didn't. Unable to connect with anyone and short tempered, he moved from job to job, leaving the United States for South America only to reappear later in San Francisco in 1860 continuing a meagre existence until the end in 1861 when the new Phineas Gage rejoined the old as his body expired.

Both Phineas and Renaud could think and could feel before and after their accidents. Both had a strong personality before and after these incidents, but both their personalities had been changed in such a way that they could no longer socially connect. As a result their decision-making capabilities were altered in a way no one could have previously imagined. But what has this got to do with followership?

Remember the suit? Our human decision-making theories imply that decision making is devoid of emotions. Armed with knowledge, followers make calculated choices (cost–benefit calculations yielding the highest incentive value) based on rational assessments of characteristics. Yet we now see that there are two issues with this. The first, as shown by the suit experiment, is the issue of time. We do not witness everyone stopping in the streets before moving, yet we would expect to do so, given the time necessary to make a reasoned argument. The second, as demonstrated by Albert and Phineas, is that despite retaining a normal intellect (perfect working memory, attention, comprehension, language skills), damage to our frontal lobes results in impaired ability to function socially. The decisions made are socially inappropriate despite being rationally sound. To think of followership decisions as resulting from a rational assessment of self-interest therefore ignores a large part of why we follow.

Despite everything we now know about how our brains work, which quite frankly is still not that much, we find it hard to accept the notion that emotions and reason are connected. The Phineases and Alberts of this world gave us our first clue that the frontal lobes are associated with our social conduct and that damage to them alters decision making. When we make decisions we not only reason, but we also feel. Our cognitive processes take a short cut that we all know as the 'gut feelings' we talked about earlier.

In fact, and to simplify for the sake of expediency (but feel free to check the science behind all of this as it is nothing if not fascinating), when we experience something we codify an emotion alongside it (a process using what are known as somatic markers).[4] The physiological attributes (sweaty palms, accelerated heart rate, facial expression...) that occur are transformed by our brains into emotions that tell us something about what we have just experienced. These emotions become associated with situations and recur when we are faced with similar decisions. This biases our decision making. When faced with a decision (eg should I follow or not?) all of these markers come together to direct our decisions and actions. These markers are processed in the ventromedial prefrontal cortex, the very section that was damaged in both our earlier stories.

Social behaviour (of which the act of following is one example) is best understood as a relationship between reason and emotion. Reason and emotion are not distinct processes with one to be cherished and one to be feared in decision making. They act in tandem in response to the stimuli we receive from our environment.

There is one more thing we need to keep in mind when looking at decision making, and if you drive you'll know exactly what I'm talking about. You too, I am pretty sure, will have had the experience of driving home back from work only to find you have arrived and aren't quite sure how that happened. You had been thinking about work, the family, the next holiday or a dreadful deadline, while your brain had been thinking about how to get you home safely. The auto-pilot was fully engaged without you even realizing it.

This is an example of the added complication for anyone trying to understand how we make followership decisions. The association between the emotions and reason that drive our choices is not always conscious. As a result, our decision-making process may occur covertly as well as overtly.

The Harvard and Boston University psychologist, the late David McClelland, demonstrated not only the importance of the unconscious in driving our behaviour but, and perhaps more importantly for our purposes, the interplay between the conscious and the unconscious.

The paradox he discovered is critical to understanding the mechanism for what I call the followership deception.

There are two ways to discover what drives people. One is to ask them to rank factors such as their need for power, achievement and so on in order of importance. The other is to tap into their unconscious by presenting them with pictures and asking them to write stories about them. The stories are then coded for imagery that relates to these factors and to see which is more prevalent.[5] The good news is that both of these methods are good at finding out what motivates people and in predicting their resulting behaviours. If someone reports a high concern for achievement, their behaviour will tend to focus on searching for ways to excel. The same is true of hidden motives. A large amount of achievement imagery incorporated in the stories written in response to pictures will predict achievement-related behaviour.

But here is the deception. The results of both tests predict behaviour, but the tests do not predict each other. Someone expressing a conscious need for achievement may not unconsciously reveal that concern and vice versa. So what's going on! Can we be both right and wrong at the same time? Is our brain playing tricks on us?

What McClelland and his team argued is that in our everyday life we express both our conscious and our unconscious needs. When we focus on a situation and give it our full attention (ie when we reason) we call upon the drivers identified with the asking method (let's call these our values as they are the things we state are important to us). However, in our everyday life, when we act, we do so following patterns of behaviour set in our unconscious motives. Our conscious mind is pretty good at taking over to remind us of what is important to us, and therefore appropriate, for as long as we are focused on conscious decision making. But our lives are too complicated for that. Many choices we make are unconscious.

The brain drives our behaviour as well as it drives our cars, with little interference from us, leaving us free to wonder were we will go for our next holiday. But what does all this matter to anyone trying to better their leadership skills? For the answer to that you will need to turn to the next chapter.

The tweet

To be effective leaders must understand why we follow and know that followers' choices are neither fully rational nor fully conscious.

Notes

1 Gobillot, E (2007) *The Connected Leader*, Kogan Page.

2 Further work on the science of cognition and emotion can be found in Joseph LeDoux's *The Emotional Brain* (Weidenfeld & Nicolson, 1998). And for all those keen on telling me 'it doesn't quite work like that,' I hope it is fair to say that whilst I have grossly oversimplified the science I do believe I have stayed true to its conclusions!

3 Which is incidentally how I came across it, by reading Pierre Bellemare and Jean-Francois Nahmias' *Crimes de sang 2* (TF1 Editions, 1992).

4 The idea of somatic markers was first proposed by Antonio Damasio in his groundbreaking (and to my mind fascinating) book *Descartes' Error* (Vintage books, 2006, first published in 1994).

5 To learn more about human motivation and the use of thematic apperception tests, a good place to start is David McClelland's *Human Motivation* (Cambridge University Press, 1988).

CHAPTER 2

EMOTIONAL LOGIC: THE FOLLOWER'S DECISION-MAKING ENGINE

Underpinning question and why it matters

How does emotional logic work?

There are two ways to be followed. One is to drag people along and the other is to attract them. As we have seen previously, decisions to follow are made by followers using a kind of emotional logic (neither fully rational nor fully emotional and neither fully conscious nor unconscious). Knowing how emotional logic works will enable us to attract others.

I have always been terrible at judging where the line one is not supposed to cross lies – especially when it comes to humour. I blame it on being French (for no other reason than I was brought up a citizen of the world, and as such, find it appropriate to follow my fellow citizens in blaming most things on the French). But even I, with my dubious sense of what constitutes funny versus rude or upsetting, could tell, on that pleasant June morning in the market town of Newmarket, England, that I had gone too far.

This was my first proper job. After the requisite training period I had finally got a position as the manager of the Newmarket branch of a large retail bank. My retiring predecessor was the last of a dying breed of bank managers.

A pillar of the local community, he was known to many and respected by all. A successful man, he had led a successful team to create a successful branch.

With hindsight I realize that this was the very reason I had been given this branch as my first posting. The team he had left behind could pretty much lead itself. The number two was more of a number one than I would ever be during my tenure there. The customers made few 'out of the ordinary' demands; most requests were ones that even the most inexperienced manager could meet. Yet, here I was, in my 20s, personally doubting my suitability for the role but trusted by my superiors (who seemed to have missed my inability to count, never mind lead) to manage a team of 10 and influence the lives of many in search of loans and savings products.

My brain possesses a default setting when nervous and that default setting is humour. Arguably, and most who know me would indeed argue, that setting is faulty, and as I found out that morning, those who know me are indeed right!

For those of you not familiar with Newmarket, it is a small, pleasant market town in Suffolk. Like so many other towns in the area, Newmarket could have been an ignored yet pretty dot on a map, were it not for its illustrious history as the global centre for thoroughbred horse racing. Dating as far back as 1174, the town developed a passion for horse racing. The frequent royal visits that ensued helped it substantiate its claim as the horse-racing capital of the world. As it has over 50 stables, five of the 35 races that constitute the British Champions series, two race courses and is the former home of the Jockey Club, there are few people in Newmarket who are not somehow connected with the sport.

So in a town that counts approximately one horse for every five human residents (3,000 of the former to 15,000 of the later), I should have known better when my new sales manager asked me 'do you like horses?' than to answer 'it depends how they're cooked'.

To me that was pretty quick witted. A prime example of a good quip spoken at the right time. To her, a keen rider and lover of all things equestrian, it was gross, inappropriate and only to be expected of a jumped up, over-promoted youngster from a barbarian country where they eat horses (rather than just shoot them if they break a leg during a race and turn them into glue as is the British preference).

The point is that humour is contextual. It is context-dependent. Had my sales manager not been so keen on horses, she might have laughed. Equally, something that is funny in one context may become normal in another. Transfer the scene to a Parisian street, in front of a Boucherie Chevaline (horse butcher) and you have a normal discussion with no humour (or upset) involved.

What made the Newmarket scene funny to me and upsetting to her was the clash of two patterns of thought, neither of which expected the other. She thought love for the animal; I thought love for the meat. Most humour is about breaking patterns of thought. The brain, surprised by an unexpected twist, rewards us with an emotional reaction (laughter – or disgust in this case).

Now let me be really clear, I do not tell this story to present myself in front of a broader jury in order to increase the odds of my humour being found appropriate. I know it was in poor taste. I simply recount it on the basis that language is about to play a key role in our story.

Even though I have never been a natural linguist and never had any great language-learning facilities, I have always loved language itself. I love its intricacies, its rhythm and rhymes and above all its ability to move us. Language knew, before our scientists did, that 'to move' was the right verb to use when describing the impact it made on us. Indeed we now know that to move us figuratively and emotionally is a precursor to moving us literally and physically. It is this ability to move us that has elevated language to the number one position in the rankings of tools for making leaders. Equally, through the spreading of rumours, the use of humour or simply the exchange of ideas, it is also the tool favoured by the oppressed to fight the oppressor.

Leaders are first and foremost orators. From our ancestors' early days of settling in social groupings, the ability to use language was seen as a key leadership trait. Be it the Western world's tendency to associate the most talkative people with leaders, or the Asian world's desire to recognize as wise those who speak little but true, we are wired to use language as a determinant of leadership status and potential. But language, in so far as it activates emotional logic, is also a fundamental tool of followership.

In Chapter 1, I made the case that it is both emotions and reason that drive our choices in a way best described by the 18th-century Scottish philosopher David Hume: 'Reason is, and ought only to be, the slave of the passions.'[1] It is this mix of emotions and reason that I called emotional logic. Even the most reasoned choice cannot be made without an emotional component. It is emotions that drive us to listen to reason. If reason is the vector to our actions, then emotions are the thrust that propel us to act. And it is language that fuels our decision making.

I promised you that our small trip through the workings of the brain in Chapter 1 had some relevance to the way followers decide who becomes a leader. So let me explain the mechanics of emotional logic. Of course, this book is written in English, so the examples I will use are particular to that language. I therefore leave it to you, or indeed potential translators, to find the ones most appropriate if English is not your first language.

Whilst Noam Chomsky, often forgotten as a key figure of linguistics due to his political presence, postulated that grammar and syntax as well as our language acquisition abilities are universal and hard-wired in our brains, the fact that we have multiple languages has always fascinated human beings. Many traditions, from sacred texts to folk cultural traditions, have sought to explain the fact that our planet doesn't (yet) have a common language.

I personally rather like the explanation offered by the Snohomish tribe of the Pacific north-west of America. It goes something like this. After witnessing a heated argument between chiefs as to whether flying ducks' noises resulted from the beating of their wings or the wind blowing through their beaks, the Sky Chief, eager to stop any escalation of the argument into violence, split them up into three tribes (on the basis that a third sub-group had no opinion). Those three tribes each created their own language and multiplied.

To understand emotional logic, let's mix the horses of Newmarket with the Snohomish duck. Here is the sentence I invite you to ponder on – the duck is ready to eat. What does it actually mean? I tested it on my children. Charlotte explained that the duck was now ready to be served having cooked for long enough whilst George disagreed, implying instead that the sentence indicated the duck had left the pond waiting for the leftover bread to be thrown at it. Both are right of course, as the sentence implicitly carries both meanings. How though do we determine what I actually meant?

As in every conversation there are three things that determine understanding: the emitter (in this case me), the receiver (my children) and the context (where the conversation takes place and what precedes it). If I am standing in the kitchen whilst hurrying the children to finish their homework to come to dinner, it is pretty unlikely that I am referring to the duck wanting our leftover bread. That is unless I am looking out of the window at our garden pond and my tone of voice changes as our pet duck is now likely to delay our dinner since it has decided at that very moment to come to our door begging for bread.[2]

In the experiment I conducted with my children however, the context wasn't giving any indications of the meaning. We were in the living room, sitting down and I explained that I wanted them to tell me what they understood by a random sentence I was about to give them. I know, I am one entertaining father! Charlotte, a keen cook, was quick to identify the sentence as an indication of cooking time whist George, devoted feeder of ducks, associated the sentence with a trip to the local pond.

What neither of them pondered however (pun indeed intended) was how they would get to a decision. Their minds decided for them. This happened at high speed.

Despite this unconscious mechanism, if we are ever asked to justify our choices (by others, or by our conscience) we are pretty clever at doing so. In fact, our brains are so adept at providing rationales that they can even quickly devise ones that cover up the irrational nature of our choices.

In their 2007 study 'The origins of cognitive dissonance: evidence from children and monkeys', published in the *Psychological Science* journal, Louisa C Egan, Laurie R Santos and Paul Bloom of Yale University highlighted some interesting findings on the way we make decisions and, perhaps more importantly, how we rationalize them. Here is how the experiment worked.

Pre-school children and capuchin monkeys were given a choice (not at the same time, in the same room, I hope for the sanity of the scientists involved!) between two equally appealing alternatives (a couple of exactly similar M&Ms). Now this is a tough choice for anyone who believes in rational decision making as the experimenters have in fact removed any rational reasons for making a choice – the two alternatives are of exact equal value.

What they expected, as psychologists versed in the workings of cognitive dissonance, and indeed what did happen, is that once the choice had been made for no rational analytical or logical reasons, the children's attitude changed towards the alternative they had rejected. They deemed it less valuable. When presented with a choice between a new option and the original unchosen option, both children and monkeys placed more value on the new option, thereby showing their disdain for an equally attractive option they had previously rejected. In a control group that did not have to make the first decision, the third option became just one more variable in a tricky choice of equally attractive options.

What we do unconsciously is wired in our brain developmentally and evolutionarily. What Egan, Santos and Bloom have done is to provide us with evidence that the mechanism needed to fulfil our need to reduce cognitive dissonance (the discomfort we feel when having to hold conflicting ideas simultaneously) is the way we rationalize the decisions hard-wired in the brains of both human and nonhuman primates. They also incidentally proved beyond doubt what I have told my children for years – they are both cheeky monkeys.

Scientists call the mechanism by which we arrive at meaning 'networks of association'. And it is these networks of association that help us understand the mechanics of our emotional logic.

Looking at why followers follow and whom they choose to follow helps us highlight the two shortfalls of leadership development strategies. The first is the assumption that by looking at the characteristics of successful leaders (as measured by their performance in their role) and developing those in ourselves we too can become better leaders. The second is the fallacy that we can identify the characteristics of great leadership by asking followers why they choose who they follow.

Like the drunk searching for his lost keys under a lamppost because that's the only place that is lit up, we focus at our peril on leaders when trying to learn about great leadership. On the face of it such a focus seems logical; after all what else would you study if not leaders? But let's take a step back.

If you go into any organization and ask who the great leaders are, you will inevitably be provided with two things – one is an organizational chart setting out the leadership roles and the other a set of key performance indicators for the leadership role holders. Great leaders will be identified as the individuals in leadership positions who deliver great results (the measures, whether hard or soft, are irrelevant to this argument).

But organizations are relatively new human constructs. In evolutionary terms they barely register in the grand scheme of things. To perform well, organizations need to be managed, and management too is a human construct. We identify people with the skills to coordinate the activities of other people. In essence management is about engineering compliance. This is a definition, not a value judgement. As our organizational life evolved we quickly saw that some people were better at inspiring compliance rather than engineering it, and called these leaders.

The point is that evolutionary psychology shows us that the idea of leadership is not the same as management. This is not because leaders inspire where managers engineer, but rather because management requires compliance where leadership requires self-direction on the part of followers.

Our ancestors followed the best hunter when it was time to hunt (their choice), or the strongest warrior when it was time to fight (their choice), or the wisest elder when it was time to resolve disputes (their choice). When was the last time anyone chose their leaders in organizations? As it turns out, this happens much more often than the HR department is aware of.

There is a discrepancy between the leaders the company identifies on a chart and the leaders followers choose to follow. In our ancestral past it was leadership, not hierarchy, that was critical for survival and leadership was what followers decided it would be. Leadership in that distant evolutionary past did not reside in a role, it resided in an individual. It was the individual who was followed for her ability to fulfil a given role. As such leadership was distributed and transient.

Over the last couple of years I have conducted the simple survey I asked you to go through in the introduction. I asked a group of around 500 managers in different organizations who the leaders they admired were. The results were not that surprising. Mandela featured heavily. Gandhi was nominated on many occasions and President Obama was there too. Wartime heroes made it onto the list (Churchill for the Brits) as did altruists (Mother Teresa). A few figures from the business world made my list (Steve Jobs, Richard Branson, Jack Welch). But only around 10 per cent of my respondents nominated someone in their company and, of those, only half chose someone they actually had reported to or were currently reporting to.

That doesn't mean organizations haven't got great leaders but it means that when people are asked who the great leaders are that they would follow, the default setting is primeval, it is self-directed and it resides in what followers call charisma, which is, as we will see later, a shorthand for emotional logic.

We are drawn to these people because of the networks of association they inspire in us, not because of the roles they have. If following is about forgoing our immediate personal goals in the pursuit of self-fulfilment (or survival), we have to feel attracted to the people we entrust with our destiny, and not simply because we have been appointed to their team.

But of course, my simple survey also contains flaws. How are we to know that these people are necessarily great or even successful? After all, human history is littered with what Jean Lipman-Blumen, in her fantastic book on followership failures of judgement, calls toxic leaders.[3] This is partly a philosophical and moral issue: if leadership is about releasing the discretionary effort of others and releasing that discretionary effort is self-directed, we will have to accept that sometimes we followers make poor choices. But this is also what we try to mitigate by looking at performance indicators. This is precisely why the question of how we choose who to follow is important. Do we look at these performance indicators in order to make the right choices? Are we rational in our choices?

And here again the answer produces a conundrum for anyone who looks at leadership development models. They are all very rational and logical. They derive causality from correlation. If x does y and is successful whilst people who don't do y aren't, then we must attribute x's success to doing y. But as we saw, that's not how our brains work. Even if x doing y is a correct observation, attributing success to it is simply post-event rationalization.

So let's agree for the time being on one fact. We choose to follow who we choose to follow because it kind of feels right. So as we progress on our journey to developing leadership greatness the next logical step is not to study leaders or to ask followers, but rather it is to understand how our emotional logic, the marriage of the emotional and the rational with the conscious and unconscious, works in making some leaders more attractive than others.

There are many drivers of behaviour. At one end sit knowledge and skills. These are the acquired and trainable tools of human conduct. We do things because we know how to do them. Our motivation, though, the reason we do the things we do, is harder to understand. As we saw in Chapter 1 it includes some fundamental, deep-seated, unconscious motives as well as acquired, semi-conscious values. These are the results of hard-wired early associations we make between events and results. Our brains are cognitive pattern-making machines. By linking reason and emotions to stimuli, our brain makes us unconsciously associate certain events with certain intellectual and emotional responses. In turn this ensures decisions can be made and taken (remember Phineas Gage and the somatic markers hypothesis in the last chapter?)

When I mentioned the duck to my children, the brain made associations and choices, quite outside my children's awareness, to come up with a satisfactory and indeed satisfying meaning. In fact the operation of these networks is so fast, complex and unconscious that I could easily have primed my children to get a specific meaning should I have wanted to. I could, for example, have asked them to watch a cookery programme before asking my question, or asked them to read the recipe for duck a l'orange. The likelihood is that this 'priming' would have made them choose the cooking meaning rather than the feeding meaning of the sentence. We therefore need to always remain conscious of the fact that emotional logic drives our decision making in a highly context-dependent way.

There are, in fact, two dimensions of context that we need to be aware of when looking at how emotional logic makes us chose leaders. One is the external dimension (ie where I am standing when I talk about the duck being ready to eat? What is the context of the conversation that comes before the sentence? Am I known as a chef or an animal enthusiast?...) The second is the receivers' internal dimension (ie are they foodies or are they animal lovers? Are they vegetarians or farmers?...) It is these two dimensions of context and their interaction that provide the priming for the emotional-logic interpretation of the sentence.

For an interpretation to arise, the sentence needs to make sense both at a cognitive level and an emotional one. For what I have called emotional logic to arise, the brain analyses all information available in any given context at both a rational and an emotional level. The process is one of activations of networks of association to narrow the possibilities in search of meaning. What do I know about the situation? Are we in the kitchen or by the pond? Is my father a cook or a zoo keeper? These questions will search the external context for relevant information.

At the emotional level another series of networks of association will be activated given a different set of questions. Do I have strong emotions of joy at seeing ducks at the pond? Do I feel a sense of revulsion at the idea of animals being killed for food? Or is it the other way around?

Both continua are equally at play when making decisions. It is that interplay that drives us to act in a certain way. Whilst it is possible to get meaning from rational networks, decision making, which requires choices to be enacted, will call into play both emotional and rational networks.

This, rather oversimplified, explanation helps us understand why leaders often find it hard to get traction for their proposed course of action. By and large we do not see these two levels as connected. Many leaders are fond of saying that they want to capture 'the hearts and minds' of people in organizations. It is the failure to recognize that 'hearts' and 'minds' are both actually 'brain' that results in the failure to engage. The idea that logic and emotions live in two separate organs is the reason we fail to understand why a boiler-proof, data-driven, inescapable and economically justifiable strategy is not immediately lauded by staff as the promised land we want them to follow us to. Rationality alone does not make a follower.

As I wrote in the introduction, the act of followership, rather than the act of being dragged along, requires two forces. Any rocket scientist, for it is indeed rocket science, will tell you that you need both a thrust and a vector. Thrust is the force necessary for movement. Vector is the field of trajectory that gives that movement direction. To have thrust without a vector is of little use if you want the rocket to travel in a certain direction, and in the same way there is a difference in organizations between activity and action. On the other hand, a vector without thrust is just a nice dream destination that will never be reached, just as a well-articulated strategy does not guarantee organizational success.

Our analysis of the environment, based on both internal and external elements of context, triggers neural and glandular responses that result in our decisions. Our emotions interact with our cognition to react and act. The patterns our brain makes as a result of both emotional and cognitive processes ensure we learn for the future. All of this happens without the need for awareness. This is why we do things because they feel right rather than merely because they are so. Emotional logic is the way by which we develop our own thrust and put in place vectors without the need for an external boost (which any form of encouragement from coaxing to coercion would be).

This is an important lesson for leaders. Followership cannot be coerced. Coercion may well secure a temporary vector (ie you will do what I say) but it has no independent thrust (you will not do anything independently of my command). As a result coercion secures effort but it does not secure discretionary effort (the difference between the level of effort required to complete an assigned task and the level of effort one is capable of). Yet it is this discretionary effort (allocated willingly and independently) that makes followership. As I said in the last chapter, when it comes to leadership, it is the follower that makes the leader. Here is a test: if you turn around and no one is behind you, you are not a leader!

The people followers are attracted to are those able to ignite their emotional logic. They are the people to whom they have an emotional as well as rational reaction. The critical step therefore in our inquiry on how to best develop as leaders is to build a working understanding (rather than a scientific description) of how emotional logic works. At its simplest, our logic when it comes to decision making happens at the cross-over of two continua: the rational–emotional and conscious–subconscious (Figure 2.1). These two continua act equally upon every decision that we take.

Figure 2.1 A 360° view of decision making

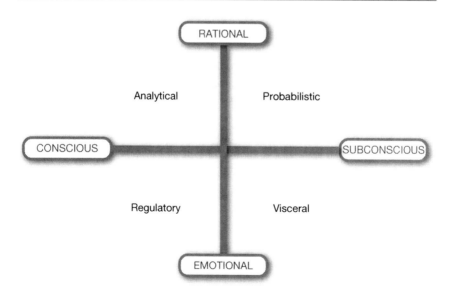

To inspire followership is to create resonance along those two continua. Igniting all four quadrants is necessary for full engagement. The 360° view explains the follower's 'it kind of felt right' explanation. The conscious analysis married with the subconscious fast probability assessment provides the 'right' whilst the subconscious visceral reaction aligned with behavioural regulation on the part of the followers provides the 'kind of felt'.

Rationally we will either analyse a situation or, as in the duck is ready to eat example, our brain will unconsciously weigh probabilities of context to come up with an answer. Emotionally we will either regulate our emotions as we think appropriate to the occasion, or unconsciously have a visceral reaction to stimuli. Followership decisions are powerful decisions. Only when the four quadrants are igniting does real engagement ensue.

There are three steps followers look at to derive this resonance. For the sake of simplicity as well as clarity, I have labelled these steps dimensions and articulated their definitions as the questions followers are asking of leaders to assess that dimension (Figure 2.2). Of course, I am very much aware that there is an apparent flaw in the way the logic works. I have been at pains to explain that emotional logic is not rational and conscious. Yet by describing the three dimensions as I have, I seem to give an impression that they are. I seem to imply that followers make a conscious, rational assessment of a leader's performance under each dimension. This is not the case. As we go through each dimension it is important to remember that followers will experience the dimension rationally and emotionally as well as consciously and unconsciously. It is also important to remember that the dimensions are not as sequential as the model implies.

Figure 2.2 The three dimensions of emotional logic

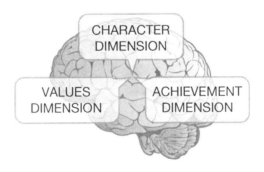

The values dimension

The first step to activating emotional logic is to create an emotionally compelling and coherent narrative for leadership. At this step followers are looking for an answer to the question: 'Does this person share my values? Do they understand me?' Again, these are not questions that can be answered purely rationally. While values may be consciously chosen (as we have seen before), the resonance a potential leader creates has also to be emotional. Without a positive answer to these questions, it is impossible to create the energy necessary to attract your followers.

The character dimension

The second step is about channelling the energy of followers towards the leader. For followers to choose a leader, a choice must be offered. There must be alternatives. This step is about polarizing choices to create maximum positive feelings towards the leader. The questions we should be looking to answer are: 'Can I look up to these people? Will they stand for those values? Do they have what it takes to stick to the values when times are tough?'

The achievement dimension

This last step reminds me of the tale of the three frogs on a log. It goes like this. There are three frogs on a log and one decides to jump. How many frogs are left on the log? The answer is three, as deciding to jump is not the same as jumping. The achievement dimension is potentially the most cognitive and rational of the three steps. It is about offering the vector to the thrust of Steps 1 and 2. Here, potential leaders have to be able to answer the questions: 'Are they capable of achieving their vision? Can they demonstrate they have what it takes to transform vision into action?' In these times of uncertainty it is appealing to try to go straight to the achievement dimension but a word of warning – without the values and character dimensions, you will have no one to jump with you to achieve anything.

Of course, models of any kind always appear neat and tidy. Leadership models in particular are always frighteningly elegant. They tend to contain attributes neatly grouped into practical steps. This is an illusion; life is not neat and tidy. It is neither linear nor sequential. So whilst I have simplified the steps for the purpose of explanation, as will become apparent throughout the following chapters, igniting emotional logic is not that sequential. There is, however, a logic to using that order in the process of description. The cognitive appeal of leaders (the achievement dimension) is a distant third in the mind of followers. Whether or not they are conscious of their impact, leaders who release discretionary effort first and foremost create emotional resonance in the brains of their followers.

Describing these three elements as steps would give an impression of sequence – after all we take one step after another or risk a fall. To address this problem I refer to these elements as dimensions. The dimension description underlines the fact that these are not steps a leader takes, but rather moments of assessment on the part of the potential follower. I can never state strongly enough the need to emphasize the role of followers in determining the success of leaders. Using the word dimension also underlines the fact that these assessments are not fully grounded theories rationally worked through and tested by followers. They can happen in a very short period of time. They can be the result of one conversation or one encounter. Whilst I realize it will always be hard to move away from any references being made to stages or steps of a model, I hope that the fact that these happen all at once at all times in the mind of followers is not lost in the discussions.

The premise of this book and what the three dimensions will demonstrate, is that rationality alone (expressed through contracts, strategies, incentives, roles and plans in today's businesses) will always fail as a sustainable leadership strategy. To truly secure the discretionary effort of followers, leaders will need to appeal to their emotional logic. This sort of premise is not an easy one to take on board in the world of work, which values rationality above emotions. It is often tagged as being either Machiavellian or soft (neither of which is intended as a compliment). Yet this refusal to work with the emotional logic of followers is a refusal to admit the science of humanity. We are attracted and devoted to leaders who create resonance in us by displaying a kind of charisma we neither quite understand nor are able to quite explain, but to which we always respond. Understanding this idea of charisma as the engine for emotional logic is essential, and this is where we will go next.

> ### The tweet
>
> Followers make choices through emotional logic, a process leaders ignite by creating resonance through emotional and rational connections.

Notes

1 David Hume, *A Treatise of Human Nature: Being an attempt to introduce the experimental method of reasoning into moral subjects* (Penguin Classics, new edition, 2004).

2 For information, I do not have any ducks nor a pond I could put them in. This is just an example. I feel the need to state this clearly for all British readers, who since the 'MPs' expenses scandal' associate ducks and ponds with unscrupulous, overpaid, dishonest people.

3 Lipman-Blumen, J (2004) *The Allure of Toxic Leaders: Why we follow destructive bosses and corrupt politicians and how we can survive them* (OUP USA).

CHAPTER 3
CHARISMA: THE ONE THING THAT MATTERS

Underpinning question and why it matters

What are the elements of emotional logic?

Ask anyone to describe the leaders they admire and follow and the word charisma is likely to come up early on in their description. Because it is neither easy to define nor clear whether one is born with it or not, charisma is one of those things development professionals don't really like. Yet the fact that it comes up so often is no surprise to anyone who understands the workings of emotional logic. Charisma is indeed the best way we have found as followers to describe emotional logic in action. It is what attracts us.

There are a number of reasons why I find the Musee du Louvre one of the most beautiful museums in the world. Being French is obviously one, but to my generation of French people the museum carries an even greater sense of wonderment.

It is the site of the first of President Mitterrand's 'grands projets' (a number of projects commissioned to give France a renewed confidence and some needed employment): the glass pyramid, which like the Eiffel tower before it was at first looked upon as a planning madness and a real eyesore only to later become a cherished landmark. It was a clear signal of modernity that stood on solid historical ground. It was the future that paid tribute to the past rather than ignoring or rejecting it.

It was the symbol of a France reclaiming its place at the avant-garde of culture. It was also the first monument from my first president. Like so many of us who had come of age for our first presidential election, I proudly claimed to belong to what his advertising genius Jacques Seguela had labelled 'Generation Mitterrand'. But you don't have to share my history to find Le Louvre a compelling place. In fact, as it is one of the world's largest and most visited art museums, it is clear I am not the only one to think this most Parisian of landmarks worth a detour. That said, a detour may not be enough to take in the fabulous collection of 35,000 objects dating from prehistory to the 19th century exhibited over some 60,000 square metres. But it is the painting collection with its 6,000 pictures I want to focus on for a moment.

Anyone visiting the Louvre for the first time could be forgiven for thinking that this vast building holds only two artefacts. Standing in the middle of the main pyramid to plan your visit you cannot help but notice signs everywhere directing you to two women – one an Ancient Greek statue of Aphrodite better known as the Venus de Milo, the other a painting of wealthy 16th-century Florentine, Lisa del Giocondo, better known as The Mona Lisa.

Whether it is the magic of signage or the desire to follow the crowd, by midday 70 people will file in every minute to pay homage to Leonardo Da Vinci's most famous painting. Any warning from me on how disappointing an experience seeing the Mona Lisa is will fall on deaf ears. No visit to Paris is complete without casting your eyes on that smile (however little you actually see of it). If you are like everybody else, you will first be surprised by how small the painting is (77 by 53 centimetres). You will then be disappointed at how far away you are from the bullet-proof glass tomb it inhabits. And finally you will get your camera out (with or without flash despite the myriad of signs telling you not to use it) and record for posterity your pilgrimage to one of the most talked about paintings of our age.

What makes the whole thing even more disturbing is that in your rush to see the famous painting you will walk past some of the greatest masterpieces ever painted including, arguably (and many art historians have argued) some paintings with at least as much historical, social and artistic significance as the Mona Lisa, which by some accounts is not even Da Vinci's greatest work.[1]

There are a number of reasons why the trip to Le Louvre is 'de rigueur' for anyone visiting Paris, but our herd instinct has to be one of the top ones. If anyone is likely to ask you about it back home, you'd better ensure you did the visit. But why this painting? Why not one of the many others on show?

Another key reason of course is the Mona Lisa's worth as a masterpiece. From the time Leonardo painted it using some of the most innovative painting and composition techniques of the time (contrapposto, stufamo and chiaro-scuro are all posh terms you may want to use at a dinner party to describe Leonardo's use of light, shade, contrast and blending), his contemporaries recognized the painting as a major shift in the history of art. Its status as a prized and priceless masterpiece also helps explain its popularity. But so too does the fact that it has been linked to so many intrigues and famous people.

That Francis I, King of France, displayed it in his palace to impress dignitaries and Napoleon Bonaparte hung it in his bedroom to impress Josephine (or any other 'dignitaries, he happened to be, entertaining') helped establish the picture as an important one. But it was the 19th-century's Romantic Movement that brought the smiling belle to the masses. Her mysterious smile and the disputed (although now settled) identity of the sitter made her the perfect femme fatale, muse to the writers' desires.

Finally, the 20th century sealed its fate as a superstar of the art world through numerous acts of vandalism, culminating in a theft involving none other than French poet Guillaume Apollinaire and painter Pablo Picasso. Add a tour of the United States starring John F Kennedy and stir a bit of Dan Brown into the mix and you have a potent recipe for attraction.

I started this chapter by mentioning the signs in Le Louvre, as if the museum were anxious to get you to see its two most popular exhibits. But the signs are not in place because the museum wants you to go there. They are there because you want to go there. That's the funny thing about signage – it doesn't actually direct people, it simply helps them get more efficiently to where they want to go. I have often walked the corridors of Le Louvre wondering how soul-destroying it would be the whole day long having to give people directions if those signs weren't there.

The Mona Lisa is indeed attractive. Indeed, as we stand in the Louvre watching visitors go by there is no doubt that it attracts countless followers. This is an attraction that is neither fully emotional nor entirely rational, one that seems as conscious as it is unconscious. But the painting also polarizes. Whether you feel it has been cheapened by over-exposure or has democratized art, you are moved to have an opinion. It is that opinion that creates the relevance of the painting. But, more importantly for us, the Mona Lisa is relevant here as it can teach us about the elements of emotional logic.

The first thing the painting teaches us is the 'whole body' nature of emotional logic. Too often we see leadership and followership as residing in the brain. We forget that the brain is connected to everything else. When trying to develop leadership it is always worth remembering the connected nature of our bodies. We gain our insights first and foremost from our senses. Sure, the Mona Lisa has now moved beyond being a painting to representing an idea, but it is its visual appeal and the visual references that accompanies this that charge us. The body is not just the vehicle that carries our brains to meetings; it is an inherent part of followership. From our early days in the savannah when we would elect to follow tall and big warriors for safety (as we saw in Chapter 1) to more intriguing recent findings about how we engage through our body, we must understand emotional logic as being about more than just neurons.

As mentioned in the last two chapters, to think that we are purely rational decision makers is as much a mistake as to think we are emotional ones. That Descartes told us to think to prove that we are was misguided but forgivable given the scientific knowledge of the time (although who am I to forgive the great man whom I am far too small to accuse in the first place). Where he was seriously wrong was to infer that the conscious brain is the sole agent in decision making. Prodding into the way we make choices should not just be about prodding (metaphorically as well as literally) into our brains. The truth is different. Decision making, it turns out, is indeed a 'whole body' event as stimuli received by the body inform the choices our prefrontal cortex make. And if you still doubt it, consider this.

Researchers from the University of Aberdeen asked blindfolded participants in turn to recall past experiences and anticipate their future lives. Having fitted participants with sensors to detect movements, they were able to prove that when people think of the past they tend to lean backwards – and forwards when imagining the future.[2]

Researchers from Tufts University and the Universities of Denver and Toronto decided to see how squeezing an object could influence our choices. They gave half their participants a soft ball to squeeze and the other half a hard ball. They showed random pictures of people whose gender was hard to categorize and asked participants if they were male or female. The participants who squeezed the soft ball decided the faces were female whilst the hard-ball group opted for male.[3]

In another example researchers from the University of Amsterdam demonstrated how when participants holding a heavyweight clipboard were asked to estimate the value of foreign currencies they overvalued the currency compared with participants holding a lightweight clipboard who tended to undervalue it.[4]

So much for the conscious, reasonable man we are so keen on modelling our economic and social theories against!

As well as reminding us that our body is one connected whole, the second lesson the Mona Lisa teaches us is the relative nature of emotional logic. The attraction of the Mona Lisa is relative in two ways.

First, it is about context. Whilst it has always been a great painting, it did not always attract the adoration it does today. Popularity comes and goes depending on context and the resonance of the painting with the time. Whilst the painting's quality may be timeless (ie it has always and will always be a great painting by all objective standards of art history), the resonance of its appeal (its attractiveness) changes with the fashions of the time. That of course should not come as any surprise, as the attracted determines the worth of the attractor.

Second, it is about culture. What is attractive in one setting can be repugnant in another. If this wasn't the case then everyone would vote for the same person at election time. And we all know that (outside what are still too many countries) this doesn't happen. The phenomenon that one leader might be hugely appealing to some, whilst loathsome to others, is also true of work. Employees loyal to one organization will easily identify with their leader against leaders of competitors.

Whilst we must take these two elements (connectedness and relativity) into account when trying to tap into the emotional logic of our potential followers; these are the very same elements that are often missing from current leadership development efforts. This is partly due to the role-based definitions of leadership we use. Whilst role definitions may be context-dependent they tend to ignore relativity. In role-based definitions followers are allocated not attracted and therefore relativity can easily be excluded. A definition based on emotional logic cannot ignore these lessons.

That's why, when asked whom we admire and asked what makes a great leader, most followers resort to charisma – a vague enough concept to make room for relativity in order to become a suitable descriptor of the force that ignites our emotional logic. You only have to open a dictionary at the definition of charisma as 'a compelling attractiveness or charm that can inspire devotion in others' to see why it's not a bad way to describe the Mona Lisa and provide a good explanation for emotional logic.

Yet, as noted in my introduction to this book, development professionals don't really like charisma. It is too vague, making it too hard to pin down the characteristics of leaders who have it. 'You know it when you see it' is a hard starting point for anyone trying to develop anything.

But perhaps more importantly for anyone trying to earn a living from leadership development, charisma is a highly dangerous concept. Etymologically, charisma is a gift, a favour bestowed by a higher power. It is not until the late 1940s that we started to apply the term to leadership. But the gift element never quite went away. We see charismatic people as being born that way and, short of calling for being born again, it's hard to see how such a gift might be developed.

Yet charisma is a very useful pointer to leadership success as it is the closest we will ever get to understanding why followers choose some people as leaders. And when we realize that charisma is indeed a gift bestowed upon leaders, not by a higher power but rather by followers, we can then see a development route.

This is why I devoted the earlier chapters to emotional logic. It is that process, with its multiple decision-making avenues and its three dimensions, that creates charisma. So the choice is simple: either we study the leader for characteristics

Figure 3.1   Charismatic approach to emotional logic ignition

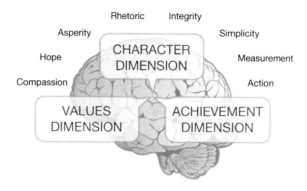

we can observe, or we study followers for choices that they make. Given that it is followers who make leaders, I know where I would rather look. And once we start to understand the workings of emotional logic using our dimensions of values, character and achievement, it becomes easy to explain what charisma means and how it can help leaders succeed.

When deconstructing the model of emotional logic it is possible to identify elements that help navigate each dimension (Figure 3.1). They are not skills or competencies but rather markers that help potential followers formulate their views.

The values dimension

As mentioned in the last chapter, Step 1 of emotional-logic ignition is the values dimension, defined as our ability to engage others emotionally. This is the first moment of truth for a potential leader – can they understand the prevailing 'mood' in the environment and articulate a way forward for followers? This step is composed of the two elements outlined below.

Compassion

Compassion seldom finds its place in the corporate dictionary. Associated as it is with some form of pity and sympathy, it is firmly confined to the 'too soft to be useful' list of emotions. Yet compassion is the starting point of leadership. Compassion drives charisma. Defining compassion only as sympathy for others' suffering is not only one-dimensional but misses the critical element of leadership – followers. Charismatic leaders are not only attuned to the current zeitgeist, they have a deep sensitivity for and thorough understanding of the needs of their followers, as well as a willingness to address them.

Hope

Understanding, however deep, is not enough to create the charge for emotional logic. Leaders must know how to use their compassion-derived insights to create hope in their followers. Whether articulated as a dream, a way forward or a strategy, the articulation of a compelling vision provides the hope necessary to make an emotional connection with potential followers.

The character dimension

Having emotionally charged potential followers, aspiring leaders need to get them to want to follow. This is the moment of truth in motivation. In this step, leaders communicate their vision in a way that inspires followership. To do so, they outline a clear choice (ie to follow or not) and make their leadership more compelling than the alternative. Of course, for most followers in corporate life there is no choice. Few organizations let followers elect their leaders. However, when it comes to the amount of effort followers put into their work there is always a choice. In the corporate world the choice may not be 'Do I follow this or that leader?' but there is still the choice of 'Do I allocate my discretionary effort to the leader or withhold it?' There are four elements that help navigate this dimension.

Asperity

Asperity is a term I borrowed from science. It is used to describe a rough edge on a surface. It is sometimes used for roughness of tone. What intrigues me about the concept and makes it relevant here is that every surface, however smooth, has a rough surface at a particle level. To ensure a choice is made, leaders also have to have a rough surface. Trying to appeal to everyone is a waste a time. Followers look for someone who appears strong in their convictions, and that strength often requires a toughness of character best described by asperity. Whilst often decried in our inclusive times, polarization is not something leaders should shy away from. Polarization is the first step of choice.

Rhetoric

But of course, asperity alone can be detrimental. Roughness does not always equal strength (in physics or life). To channel that roughness, leaders use rhetoric. From Chapter 1 onwards, I have made the point of how key language is to leadership. Leaders are orators. Words are the tools of leadership. Communication is the way leadership is expressed. To meet the needs of the character dimension you have to articulate the choices followers need to make. To be effective this articulation needs to be both emotional and rational. This is where the art of rhetoric comes in.

Integrity

In the context of emotional logic I use integrity not so much in the sense of being honest but more in its true sense of consistency and wholeness. When we are attracted to leaders we do not decide they are honest on the basis of our experience with them (remember we make followership decisions at a fast unconscious rate as well as a slow reasoned one). Rather, we are attracted by the alignment between what we perceive as what they think, what we hear as what they say and witness as what they do. That consistency is what creates the trust necessary for potential followers to give up some of their freedom to act for the benefits of followership.

Simplicity

It is clear that the way a vision is presented directly affects the motivation of potential followers. One of the key elements of emotional logic in igniting the energy of followers is simplicity. By simplicity I mean the ability to create a coherent picture of the proposed vision however complex each of its elements might be. This is best done through the creation of a narrative in which potential followers see themselves.

The achievement dimension

Having successfully navigated the first two dimensions, aspiring leaders galvanize their followers to action. The pull felt by this attraction needs to be channelled towards continued attachment. The leader shows the way forward. This step is about deconstructing the choice made into actions to be taken. There are two elements that are critical to a successful navigation of this last dimension.

Measurement

The first element is measurement. The leader needs to offer some means to measure progress along the road. This will ensure that the alignment to the vision is maintained. By measurement I do not necessarily mean metrics and targets. Rather I mean a roadmap against which followers can align their efforts. Some may use a plan whilst others may use benchmarks. What matters is that followers can measure their actions as well as assess the leader to ensure they are kept motivated by the journey.

Action

Finally, the last element I will look at is action. Leadership is not simply about painting pictures and making speeches, however attractive and grand. Leadership is about the achievement of objectives. Potential leaders become leaders by appealing to the emotional logic of followers through the vision they paint, but without actions to fulfil that vision they are quickly viewed as charlatans. This is the last step but also the first (and this is why the model is fundamentally cyclical). Things change through actions. An environment is never static. It is through actions that leadership can be as lost as fast as it can be gained (remember how quickly the wave of hope politicians create when they get elected vanishes in the face of the struggle of office). Actions are the means to achieve but also, by being the proof point of values, they are the springboard to recharge leaders.

In the following chapters I will look at each of these elements in turn and offer some advice and tools on how each can be refined and developed. It is not a coincidence of course that the initials of the above elements spell charisma. It is nevertheless more than a neat mnemonic. I have not chosen the words simply to fit the model. Each of these elements is one of the building blocks of a new definition of charisma. That definition sees charisma as the outcome of a process of emotional-logic ignition. It is charisma that is the one thing great leaders have. I am not describing charisma here as some kind of exuberant, extrovert superstar quality. Rather, charisma is an all-encompassing way to relate to the emotions and the logic of followers. Charisma is a gift from followers and many a leader has had charisma given by a set of followers that would not meet the classic definition for another group.

Before we close this chapter to continue on our journey, it is worth sounding a note of caution. This isn't an alarm as such – that would be too dramatic;

instead it is more of a warning softly spoken by the little voice in your head. The warning is this: attraction is not the same as effectiveness. To look at how leaders gain followers makes no allowance for the direction travelled by the coupled forces. It makes no room for morality. There is no morally good or bad leadership in a charismatic emotional-logic model. Leadership in and of itself is relative. It is the leader's intent that gives it direction and moral adequacy.

I am often asked if I think Hitler (feel free to replace him with any other destructive, unsavoury and all-round toxic name you care to mention) was a great leader. As one who makes a living out of studying and developing leaders and whose family directly suffered at the hands of the regime Hitler sought to establish, I always find the question worthy of an answer.

In so far as he exerted influence over others and got their discretionary effort aligned to his objectives (there are many examples of followers going beyond what was asked of them, not least in my own country of origin), there is no doubt that Hitler displayed great leadership. If we, however, imbue the word great with a sense of morality, then all bets are off. Of course Hitler was morally repugnant and his regime abhorrent, but these are reflections on his lack of humanity rather than an inadequate leadership.

This is not a rhetorical point as it goes to the heart of leadership development. Many inspiring leaders struggle with the need to somehow 'follow a recipe' whilst retaining a sense of authenticity. They feel Machiavellian. They worry about losing their integrity. Given that I am here advocating making an emotional appeal to, often unconscious, emotions, that risk is felt to be even stronger by many. Am I advocating manipulation? Am I advocating deception?

First, let me make a point that may appear flippant but isn't. Irrespective of how careful, well intentioned or clever you are, all interactions are manipulative. To the people who say they hate politics in organizations, meaning that they hate having to convince, cajole or appeal when 'the facts should speak for themselves,' I say facts are mute. Life is politics because cognition is both rational and emotional. Data are key but dissonant. Our brain gives this resonance through emotional logic by being both rational and emotional. What makes manipulation undesirable is the intent of the agent doing the manipulation, not manipulation itself (we all try to manipulate our children to keep them away from danger).

I am not advocating lying nor am I advocating deceiving. I am advocating making a message you believe in and care for resonant through an understanding of emotional logic. In that way, being a great leader is not the same as being a great man. Charisma does not define character.

Leadership development is called development and not creation for a reason. Developing something assumes something exists to be developed. It assumes something is taken to another level. That something is you – your character, your personality, your sensibilities, the shaded, nuanced and complex mix of characteristics that makes you who you are. To quote (or maybe paraphrase as I am not sure when and how he first said it) London Business School's Rob Goffee, leadership development is about 'being yourself, more, with skill'.

To develop charisma (which I will define at length by breaking it down into constituent parts) is not about trying to become Steve Jobs, Barack Obama or Mother Teresa (once again feel free to add or delete names on this list). It is to become a resonant version of you who will attract other people. The human capacity to detect inauthenticity is huge. We have an inbuilt phoney detector. But unfortunately for us, we also have an instinctive need to follow the crowd. These two elements will sometimes work against each other.

To be resonant requires authenticity. Now whether you are authentically bad, undesirable, criminal or toxic is not something I can address within the confines of leadership development. If we stopped developing tools for effectiveness because they could be abused by repugnant characters, the history of human progress would be rather short and, I for one believe, sadder for it.

All this does not, however, preclude that, at times through a development journey, we may be uneasy about some of the steps we believe we are supposed to take. Whatever skill we try to develop, we will be hesitant and mistaken on our journey to greatness. I will turn at the end of this book to some ideas on how you may make the journey easier but make no mistake, this is a journey that you alone can make.

People assume that climbing the corporate ladder requires you to leave your opinions behind and adopt those of your bosses. To do so means you quickly lose the ability to develop the very opinions that will make you a success if you reach the top. It will also mean that somewhere along the road you will have lost the one thing that makes followers want you – your charisma. So never forget that the process of leadership development is the process of trying to be who you want. That means that the first choice you have to make is to want to be a leader. Having made that choice I truly believe anyone can face a development journey. Will any of the steps and elements above make toxic leaders any less toxic? Frankly I doubt it. But the important question is: will they help you become who you want to be? I hope so, as I'm pretty sure that who you want to be deserves that chance. Let's face it, I doubt toxic leaders would take the time to read a leadership book, sure as they are of their superiority.

That being said let's start our journey through each of the elements of charisma.

The tweet

Followers' emotional logic is ignited through charisma – Compassion, Hope, Asperity, Rhetoric, Integrity, Simplicity, Measurement, Action.

Notes

1 That title is given to a number of paintings but seems to land most often on the Lady with an Ermine, the wonderfully preserved painting exhibited in Krakow's Czartoryski Museum.

2 Miles, L, Nind, L and Macrae, C (2010) 'Moving through time', *Psychological Science*, **21** (2), pp 222–23.

3 Slepian, M, Weisbuch, M, Rule, N and Ambady, N (2011) 'Tough and tender: embodied categorization of gender', *Psychological Science*, **22** (1), pp 26–28.

4 Jostmann, N, Lakens, D and Schubert, T (2009) 'Weight as an embodiment of importance', *Psychological Science*, **20** (9), pp 1169–74.

PART TWO
THE VALUES DIMENSION

The first step in igniting the emotional logic of potential followers is to fulfil the values dimension. There are two things followers assess during this first step. The first is the potential leader's ability to know what it is like to be a follower. This is characterized by questions such as: 'Do they share my values?', 'Are they my kind of people?', 'Would I share a drink with them?' The second is the ability of the leader to use that understanding to paint a picture of how things would be better under their leadership. The questions that need to be answered in this second part focus on: 'Can they do something for me?', 'What vision do they have for the future?', 'What do they set out to do?'.

The two headings that best capture what is at stake here by way of demand from followers are Compassion and Hope – the two first letters of the word charisma.

The values dimension of emotional logic

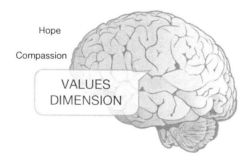

Hope

Compassion

VALUES
DIMENSION

CHAPTER 4
COMPASSION

Underpinning question and why it matters

Why does compassion matter and how do you develop it?

The first step of the values dimension is the creation of an emotionally resonant vision. Creating emotional resonance requires a deep understanding of the needs of potential followers. Compassion is the starting point to charisma. Not only because it provides us with the first letter of the mnemonic but also because it is only when they feel deeply understood that followers can give the gift of charisma to potential leaders. Building this understanding and having a strong urge to act on it is what compassion is about.

There are really only two kinds of people in the world – Excel people and PowerPoint people. Think about it. You can easily split all your colleagues, friends, family and acquaintances into those two groups.

In the Excel group sit the numbers people. The ones who think through logic and sequences. They are the ones who put together to-do lists, and they always plan in minute detail before taking action. They are the scientists, engineers, accountants and technicians.

In the PowerPoint group sit the conceptual people. They are the ones who think in pictures and have points of view driven from their guts rather than arguments that come from their rational brain. They are the artists, the dreamers, the visionaries and the marketeers.[1]

You may also want to introduce a third group – let's call these the Word people.[2] This group includes people who translate things from one group to the other. They are the catalysts and connectors, the ones who take the ideas from Excel and make them sing for the PowerPoint people. But, in truth, this is probably not necessary.

Of course this is an oversimplification. It's a false dichotomy. It's nonsense of the highest order. In fact I could have chosen two random, similarly seemingly opposed, words to describe the people you know. I could have chosen to talk about the meat versus the vegetable people or the reds versus the blues, or circles versus triangles and so on and so forth. The truth is it doesn't seem to matter what classification you choose; once you rest on one, the whole world seems to fit within it (with a few exceptions we all like because they serve to prove our new-found rule).

Even without such a flight of fancy, I could have stuck to the categorizations we use in our everyday life all the time. We talk about left-brain and right-brain people. We talk about parent and child behaviours. We oppose feminine to masculine forms of leadership. More sophisticated models might well include more variables like the MBTI profiles, whilst more populist ones might call on astrology underpinned by 12 zodiac signs or 12 Chinese animals. What they all have in common is oversimplification and some element of truth.

To describe the brain as functioning along two hemispheres, or to allocate a set of behaviours to one gender, is flawed. Whilst science has proven these overly simplistic categorizations to be wrong, there is no denying that they are rooted in some element of truth. Whilst both sides of our brains are indeed involved in processing both conceptual and analytical thoughts, it is also true that the right side of the brain recalls overall experiences whilst the left side recalls details. The same is true of gender differences. Females tend to communicate differently from males both verbally and visually.[3]

The appeal of elevating some grains of truth into universal principles is easily explained by our need to use classifications to establish the patterns we rely on to navigate the world. These patterns, once established, are incredibly difficult to shake off. Even though I completely made up the Excel versus PowerPoint people, you may still find it an attractive way to explain why cousin Bob, a clear 'PowerPointer', always frustrates cousin Betty, an 'Exceller' by birth.

There is an important reason why we value these patterns – they help us survive. Michael Shermer, publisher of *Sceptic* magazine and author of *Why People Believe Weird Things*, calls this phenomenon 'patternicity' (a more generic form of what scientists call apophenia, the experience of seeing patterns in meaningless data). The idea is simple.

Say you hear the rustling of the grass in the African Savannah. You can either assume it's the wind or a venomous snake. If you are right first time and it is the wind and you walk along, you are safe. If it was a snake, however, and you assumed it was the wind, you are dead. The pattern that will save your life is the pattern of 'rustling grass equals snake equals danger'. Provided the alternative is of lesser value (ie it cost little to assume it's a snake even if it is the wind), the pattern becomes established. Our brain is a pattern-making machine. In a world of complex social interactions, however, the line between life-saving patterns and mindless shortcuts can be paper thin.

The values dimension calls for us to create emotional connections. To do so requires a deep understanding of followers. This is where shortcuts become dangerous. A deep understanding cannot be based on some elements of truth, it has to be born out of a clear assessment. What our liking for patterns tells us is that to create this understanding, we need to be able to assess our followers' needs by understanding our own biases (ie are we clear this is about them rather than our patterns?). Enter compassion.

At its roots compassion is about emotionally connecting with (not just intel-lectually understanding but emotionally feeling) and wanting to alleviate someone else's suffering ('com' meaning with and 'patient' one who suffers). Most of us, psychologists included, tend to define compassion rather vaguely. It sits alongside empathy and sympathy, if not in the dictionary at least in the way we describe the feelings it arouses in us. It is, however, quite possible to distinguish between empathy, sympathy and compassion if we pause a moment to consider the feelings associated with each. It is also critical to make the distinction, as leaders will only be effective in meeting the require-ments of the values dimension if they can deliver on all three aspects.

Empathy is primarily about experiencing (possibly mirroring) others' feelings. These feelings can be ones of joy as well as sorrow. Pity on the other hand (more often associated with business than the others) is about judging others' feelings of suffering as weakness. It is a judgemental state in which the person experiencing pity will feel superior.

Sympathy is closer to compassion in that it deals with sorrow and pain. Unlike pity and more like empathy, it assumes an equality on the part of the person experiencing sympathy towards the other. However, it is about feeling the sorrow the other person experiences.

Compassion is different from empathy in that it deals primarily with feelings of sorrow rather than joy. However compassion contains, at its core, the desire to alleviate the suffering of the other. This is why compassion is the starting point to igniting emotional logic. Compassion calls for the leader to want to take an active role in changing the conditions for their followers.

The problem with working with compassion is that for too many people it conjures up images of Mother Teresa working with the world's poorest in the Calcutta slums, or Florence Nightingale alleviating the atrocities of war under the light of her lamp. This seems far removed from business leadership. Indeed the very notion of alleviating suffering may be difficult to handle, depending on the business you are in. So before we go too far down the road of the ills of the human condition, let me reframe the definition in a way that shows what is at stake here.

The reason compassion is dismissed so easily, in business in general and leadership in particular, is rooted in fundamentally flawed models of power. We see power as something to be acquired or gained at the expense of others. Gaining it means manipulating and demeaning others (for someone to go up someone else must go down). We see power as gamesmanship (hence we talk about power play or power games). We equate leadership and power with coercion and force. This view leads us to believe that leadership is gained. Yet, my contention so far, underpinned by years of psychological and sociological observations, is that, in fact, leadership is given not gained.

Leadership is given to the leader by followers, not gained by the leader at the expense of others. To ignite emotional logic means to attract followers (ie getting power through the impact you have on them, rather than the direct actions you take to gain it). Power is no longer about force but about the ability to change a person's condition or perception. This sets influence in direct opposition to coercion. With coercion we do not change opinions, we actively devalue and punish them. This is why compassion rather than coercion has to be the starting point of leadership.

To understand how compassion works as an element of the values dimension and to see how it addresses the issues of understanding and power raised above, it is worth turning to Abraham Maslow (of pyramid of needs fame).

Most of our understanding on the psychology of compassion is based on deficit models. Either the compassionate person has a deficit (they have to somehow fulfil a need in search for self-gratification) or the people experiencing the suffering have a deficit (they need their suffering alleviated and are unable to do so alone). It is this deficit base that leads to compassion being perceived as either weak (pitiful people coming together) or wicked (the search for self-aggrandizement). In his work, Maslow started not from a deficit model but from a surplus model. As he put it: 'It is as if Freud supplied us the sick half of psychology and we must now fill it out with the healthy half.'[4]

His starting point was to study people who had achieved unqualified success in their fields. He described those people as operating with peak experiences. Some of the people he studied were well known to him and famous to us (Abraham Lincoln, Thomas Jefferson, Albert Einstein, Eleanor Roosevelt, Benedict de Spinoza and Aldous Huxley), and others less so. What they all shared was that they were what he called 'reality-centred' rather than 'self-centred'. They were able to distinguish between reality and assumptions. They were also 'problem-centred' in that they had an insatiable thirst for solutions. This summarizes best what compassion means in the context of leadership.

The importance of reality in defining compassion cannot be overstated. It enables us to deal with the issue of 'patternicity' identified at the beginning of this chapter. By being reality-centred we focus on the actual needs of potential followers rather than our filtered view of what these may be. There are therefore two sides to the compassion element that leaders must work on.

One is understanding their own filters and patterns so they become reality-centred. The other is a willingness to act to serve the real needs identified.

Compassion contains at its core our ability to understand intellectually how others feel. I call this intellectual empathy. This is a start but, in and of itself, does not create compassion. In fact knowing how others feel can lead to the exact opposite. We may be tempted to exploit their feelings in order to manipulate them. The other pitfall is that being able to recognize an emotion does not enable you to know its source. Say you intellectually recognize that I am angry. That tells you something about my state of mind but nothing about where that state of mind comes from. I could be angry with you for what you just did or angry with my children for what I have just remembered they did last night. Understanding is critical but not sufficient. This is where the next step, emotional sympathy, comes in.

What I call emotional sympathy (I am stressing the I not out of self-aggrandizement but rather to signal that this is not a universally applicable or accepted definition of sympathy) is our ability to feel what another person feels. This ability helps us to be emotionally aligned to others. By feeling what they feel we can move beyond intellectual detachment. Just like intellectual empathy, however, emotional sympathy is not immune to drawbacks. Imagine being a leader in a crisis. You see the people around you in distress, and through intellectual empathy understand that distress. Now imagine going to the emotional sympathy stage and actually feeling that distress. What happens next? Well if you react like others faced with deep distress the answer is: nothing. And nothing might not be what your followers are looking for from you. So whilst emotional sympathy enables you to connect to your followers, it is not enough. To become a leader requires another step, which I call active compassion (Figure 4.1).

Figure 4.1   The three building blocks of compassion

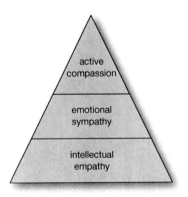

The point of active compassion is that it marries the advantages of intellectual empathy (you understand the feeling) with the benefits of emotional sympathy (you feel the predicament others are in) without falling for the pitfalls of manipulation (using others' feelings for your own ends), over-attachment (feeling like others makes you unable to act) or over-detachment (the detachment necessary not to fall for the pitfall of emotional sympathy). Active compassion is about knowing and feeling what others feel but being driven to do something to change these feelings. It is active compassion that drives potential leaders never to accept the status quo and constantly to challenge their environments (the reality and problem-focused mindsets I talked about earlier). It is what enables them successfully to navigate the values dimension by demonstrating to potential followers that they share their values. But if the process is to move through those three stages, how are we to do it?

Stage 1: developing intellectual empathy

A senior executive in a global corporation I had been invited to consult with told me the story of his friend's retirement. As a student from a modest family, my client had worked part time at a greengrocer's in his local town. Last year, the owner of the store decided to retire. To mark the occasion and express their thanks, all the students who had worked there got together and agreed to go back to the store and all to work the last day of opening before taking the owner out for dinner. It was one of those momentous emotional days when you reconnect with your past, those you promised to keep in touch with but never really did and those who gave you a push along your life.

Over dinner, my client, by now a successful and expatriated executive, was chatting to his old friends, most of whom still lived in the same town. At the end of the meal he turned around to his friends and said his goodbyes with the promise that next time they were in London they had to look him up to go for a drink together. And this is the point of the story. All looked back at him with a strange expression on their face.

This is the moment he says he realized how deep in the bubble he was now living in. You know that bubble presidents talk about when they become excluded from the real world. To my client, who spends hours on planes travelling the globe on business, the phrase 'when you're next in London be sure to look me up' is the 'how are you today' of the business world. In his world it is as common to bump into someone in the executive lounges of the world's airports as it is to common to most people to bump into someone they know in their local store.

To his friends, who travelled at best once a year out of the country on a vacation, the sentence was one of those only either a show-off looking to demean them, or a man who had left them behind, would utter. As my client is definitely not the former, he chose to remember and recall this story to encourage himself and those around him to remember that their reality is not how most of the world lives.

This is a critical realization without which intellectual empathy is not possible. We all live in a bubble created from our circumstances. For leaders this is even more the case as power increases the size of the bubble. Leaders are treated differently by their entourage. In extreme cases this leads to them forgetting the bubble exists.

The bubble causes two developmental needs. The first is the need to check our sense of what others experience against the reality of what they actually experience. The second is to clarify that understanding against the source of the expression of the feeling we see (knowing that the angry look they give is definitely a sign of anger is not enough; we need to understand where that anger comes from).

To help with seeking intellectual empathy I offer three small steps. Of course I recognize that it is easier to write and read them than it is to enact them. I am also fully aware that what can be described in about 500 words requires a lot more thought, detail and steps to be successfully concluded. I do however hope these small introductory steps open up your desire for further inquiry.

The first step is to get familiar with observable reality (ie what are you actually seeing?). The second step is to check the expression of the behaviour (ie is what you think you are seeing actually what it is?) and finally Step 3 is about checking the source of the behaviour (ie where does what you see come from?). Taken together these steps should help you progress towards intellectual empathy.

Step 1: remove yourself from the bubble (the observable reality)

In order to fight our patterns and filters and be reality-focused, we must first remove ourselves from our bubbles. Countless studies have shown that the higher up you go in an organization, the more you talk. It is a rather straightforward logical step to assume that the more time you devote to talking the less time you will devote to listening!

We make a false assumption that watching and listening are passive activities (how often do you hear watching TV held as the best example of a sedentary, passive lifestyle). But if we genuinely listen and truly watch (like anthropologists in our own tribes), we become the active observers – and without that, action will not be possible. Without listening we will never tap into the observable reality we may decide to act to change. Don't listen and you will either not change anything or, maybe worse still, change the wrong thing.

Step 2: check your understanding of the behaviour others display (the expression)

Checking our understanding of how someone feels is not easy. Picture the scene. You walk into the office in the morning and say the customary 'How are you?' to a colleague, who replies with the customary 'I'm good thanks.' However before they get a chance to move on you stop them and say with your coaching voice and accompanying concerned look: 'No. I mean genuinely, how are you this morning?'

I guess, unless you work on the west coast of the United States, your colleague's 'weirdo alert' neurons start firing up. So how can we check how people feel without being weird? The answer as always is that it depends on your starting point. If you're the kind of person who has never spoken about emotions before, this will of course be harder than if you had, but I am not talking here about running some kind of psychotherapy session.

The best way to start is to have data-driven conversations. So start sentences with: 'When you say... am I right in thinking you mean...' or better still, the best way to get to understand someone's feelings is to explain your own. 'When you say this... that makes me feel...' This kind of conversation is hard, but the more concrete you make it the safer it sounds. That said though, safety, or rather the lack of it through exposure, makes this hard and this is the reason for Step 3.

Step 3: clarify where the behaviour comes from (the source)

Knowing how someone feels is not the same as knowing why they feel that way. Of course checking with someone seems to be the best way, but add to that the fact that sometimes we don't even know why we feel the way we do and we have a challenge on our hands. Indeed there is also a question of privacy (have you got the right to even ask and potentially invade someone's privacy?). Yet clarifying where feelings come from is necessary to compassion (as without it action may be misdirected).

The best way is to have non-invasive conversations. These are conversations that leave the other party free to participate or not. The kind of question you may want to ask is 'I can see you look stressed about this; is something bothering you?' When you make the feeling concrete and open, the question comes across as an offer of help rather than a demand for explanation.

As we have seen in the first part of this book, we act on the basis of what we know and what we feel. Having developed a knowledge of what people feel does not tell us how they are likely to act on the basis of those feelings. To know that we too must experience those feelings. This is why the next stage of compassion – emotional sympathy – is critical.

Stage 2: developing emotional sympathy

As we saw above, expressing emotions is a difficult thing. Ask someone how they feel and, more than likely, they will tell you what they think. In Stage 1 we saw how if we are not fluent in expressing our own emotions it is unlikely we will be fluent in recognizing those of others. But actually the truth is even more complex than that: we are not very good at understanding our own emotions so what chance have we got of feeling the ones others feel?

As it turns out, we have a pretty good chance. Intellectual empathy is based on one way we understand people's emotions. That way is primarily visual. We see someone's face and their posture and deduce from these how they may feel. I have called this intellectual because at this stage we can be detached from the emotion (we know but don't feel). However there is another system at play and this is the one that underpins what I call emotional empathy.

Over recent years, scientists have looked at what they call sensory motor mapping of emotions. That is to say that witnessing an emotion can trigger the same emotion in the person observing it. Using brain imaging techniques it is possible to see that when someone observes an emotion, areas of the observer's brain light up that are the same as in the person experiencing the emotion. We seem to have a direct mapping mechanism for emotions. This mirror mapping of emotions is critical to our social lives. Of course like all recent discoveries there is still much speculation as to how what are commonly referred to as mirror neurons operate, but the scientific consensus appears to be that these mirror neurons are critical to our understanding another person and learning new skills (be they emotional or not), as the very exposure to someone else's emotions triggers in us similar states.

This of course does not mean that being able to experience someone else's emotions directly leads to compassion or altruism. If we experience pain by witnessing someone else's pain, we may want to get rid of the pain by helping them but may also want to get rid of it by getting rid of them. There is however something important here for us to note, which is that we are wired for compassion and as such it is not a weakness but a necessary condition for our well-being. The reason this matters is that, to be a leader, we must recognize and value our own and other people's emotions.

There is an exercise that can help that I have borrowed from a client over the last year. It's more a game than an exercise. My client calls it a 'a hat full of emotions'. We pass a hat amongst participants that is full of cards. On each card is the sentence 'Tell us about the last time you felt...' followed by an emotion (fearful, angry, impatient, proud, loved...) Don't worry if this kind of exercise engenders a strong feeling of dread in you – it does in me too, which, in this case I grant you, is the advantage of being the consultant rather than the participant! The point of these exercises is that they force us to get in touch with what different emotions mean. They sharpen up our neurons if you will.

We have in so many ways learnt the art of concealment when it comes to our emotional lives. Some of these tactics are necessary to social harmony.

Call them politeness. If your hosts ask if you are enjoying the dinner they have prepared for you, to tell them that you feel disgust at their filet mignon is bad form. Others are the result of our education – the numerous 'don't do this' and 'be strong' instructions we get from our teachers or parents. But wherever it comes from, this concealment stands in the way of our building the strong emotional vocabulary we need for a balanced emotional life at least and leadership at most.

Being able to recall emotional experiences enables us to recognize these emotions in others but it is also the trigger for them. This emotional awareness enables us to move to the next stage of compassion.

Stage 3: developing active compassion

I am pretty sure I'm not the only one. You are on a plane ready for take-off. The crew has asked you to buckle your seat belts and switch off your phones. You start to feel the plane moving towards the runway and know you are minutes away from take-off. Suddenly you spot the person next to you. They are doing a poor job of shielding their blackberry from view as they continue to type an e-mail. You are concerned. How dare they. They may or may not be right to dismiss the dangers of cell technology in planes but rules are rules and why take the risk anyway? Surely no amount of e-mail is more important than life. You are worried and furious but like every time this happens you will do nothing but hope they see sense. You might glance sideways a couple of times hoping they get the message, but whether they do or not the likelihood is that you will sit there and hope for the best.

This kind of inaction is not rare. You are not alone. It is also the reason I chose to call Stage 3 active compassion as, whilst we may recognize the need to take action, taking it is never easy. This type of behaviour is often referred to as the bystander effect.

Psychologists John M Darley and Bibb Latané conducted research into this effect following a number of cases of witnesses not taking action even when lives were at stake (most famously the case of Kitty Genovese who was murdered in plain view of a reported 38 witnesses).[5] It is hard not to be outraged by these cases. As moral human beings the easiest thing to do is to look for the inhumanity in the witnesses. This explains their behaviour and shelters us from thinking that we could ever be like them. There must be something wrong with their personality or their upbringing.

Psychologists tend to say that our behaviour is a function of our personality and the situation in which we find ourselves. Surely, in a similar situation our personality would make us do the right thing, or does some social–psychological factor associated with the situation actually matter. This, in fact, is the very dimension Darley and Latané set out to study.

They staged a pretty incredible experiment. In their study, they had a participant sit in a cubicle, from which they were instructed to speak with other participants in separate cubicles, unseen by them, about college life. The microphone would be switched on when it was their turn to speak and off at all other times so no one could hear them when it wasn't their turn.

What they did not know is that actually there was no one else involved in the study. All the other so called participants were recorded tapes. One of those on tape, early in the study, as part of his narrative on life at university mentioned that he suffered from seizures and that these made life difficult for him. As the study progressed, every time his turn would come, his voice would become louder, at times incoherent. Eventually with gasps and chokes, he asked for help as a seizure was coming on.

What Darley and Latané wanted to test was the reactions of the participants. Would they leave the cubicle (which they had not been instructed they mustn't do) to call for help? What happened next tells us a lot about ourselves. When they had been told that only two people were participating in the experiment (ie them and the seizure sufferer), the vast majority of people came to the rescue. In fact some 85 per cent of people chose to help. But as Darley and Latané increased the numbers of suggested participants, the results started to change. With three participants the figure of those who helped went down to 60 per cent, With six people supposedly involved this became as low as 30 per cent. That's right: when we believe four other people are witnesses to what we see, a good 70 per cent of us decide to do nothing.

This led Darley and Latané to their finding, which they call 'diffusion of authority'. When we think there are other witnesses we feel less personally involved. A problem shared is indeed a problem halved to the point we no longer see it as a problem. So when we sit on the plane witnessing an act we are drawn to inaction by two powerful forces. One is our culture (we don't want to make a fuss); the other is diffusion (surely someone else will pick it up, and more importantly the people whose job it is will). These two forces do stand in the way of us taking the next stage of compassion, which is action. So what can we do to prevent inaction?

Step 1: connection

What Darley and Latané showed is that there are strong situational elements rather than personality types that help or hinder action. One of the interesting elements of the bystander-effect studies is that when the group is connected, people are more likely to take action (this may be because connections will attenuate the cultural drawbacks linked to intervention). For a leader this means fostering a culture of emotional connections among followers. By openly talking about your feelings and encouraging others to do the same you will build a more compassionate culture.

Step 2: recognition

To do anything though, you must witness the event and recognize it is one in which help is needed. This is why I split compassion into three stages. Intellectual empathy and emotional sympathy underpin active compassion. If you are blind to the needs of others, you will be mute when it comes to action. You will recall that when defining intellectual empathy I offered a checking step. The reason is that one of Darley and Lantané's findings was that when we are unsure of ourselves or where the situation is ambiguous, we are less likely to act. To act we must see something as a problem. Recognizing others' emotions is the start to acting on them.

Step 3: cognition

The final step however is cognition. What I mean by that is quite simple: by knowing about the bystander effect you are more likely to protect yourself from it. We are wired for compassion; even if some social norms try to curtail that instinct, it is one that we have. None of the participants in the bystander effect study actually made the decision *not* to help. They were all conflicted. They wanted to help but the fear of standing out, being in danger, interfering or being mistaken prevented them from doing so. By making a conscious choice to choose a compassionate mindset we reveal our urge to help. This may seem a bit trite in the face of such powerful notions as the bystander effect but by being more conscious and accepting of our and others' emotional lives, we can be more powerful as leaders.

Let's recap where we are. To become a leader we must ignite the emotional logic of others. Igniting emotional logic is about successfully navigating three dimensions. The first of these, the values dimension is about creating emotional connections by painting a compelling, resonant vision. The second, the character dimension, is about guiding these emotional connections towards choosing that vision. The third, the achievement dimension, is about the fulfilment of that vision. Whilst compassion is the first step of the values dimension, potential followers will only see a potential leader as being worth their commitment if they can create a complementary set of emotions to the ones shown through compassion. That complementary set is the emotions that differentiate a fellow follower (ie someone we want to associate ourselves with because they understand us) from a leader (someone we want to follow because not only do they understand us but they also paint a picture of how much better we can be). This set of emotions falls under the heading 'hope' and this is where we are going next.

The tweet

Compassion is a leader's call to action. It is made up of intellectual empathy + emotional sympathy + active compassion.

Notes

1   To the Mac people, I urge you not to translate this categorization across to Numbers and Keynote people as it doesn't work as well, given Numbers' ability to turn numbers into pictures!

2   Or Pages people for Mac folks.

3   For some of the best writing on the state of 'brain science' for the non-scientist I would highly recommend John Medina's brilliant *Brain Rules: 12 principles for surviving and thriving at work, home and school* (Pear Press, 2008).

4   Maslow, AH (1968) *Toward a psychology of being*, Van Nostrand.

5   Darley, JM and Latané, B (1968) 'Bystander intervention in emergencies: diffusion of responsibilities', *Journal of Personality and Social Psychology*, **8** (4), pp 337–83.

CHAPTER 5
HOPE

Underpinning question and why it matters

What is the place of hope in leadership and how do we create it?

Given that our need for leaders is born out of our need for reassurance, there can be no more important a concept in leadership than the concept of hope. Hope is the output of compassion. When followers consider the values dimension by asking themselves (albeit somewhat unconsciously) 'Does this person share my value?' the positive answer they seek determines how hopeful they can be about their own future and therefore how attractive the leader will be.

If the fall of 2006 saw the book become number one on both the New York times and Amazon.com's bestseller lists, it was in the winter of 2007 that the movement took prominence. By one of those quirks of good fortune, the timing of *The Audacity of Hope*, the second book by the ascending Senator Barack Hussein Obama, couldn't have been better. For us, trying to understand the second element of charisma, it is not so much the book or its message that is key here but rather the way it helped a relatively unknown senator to become a president. In our charisma model hope comes early as it explains why people decide to follow as we saw in Chapter 1. The story of *The Audacity of Hope* helps us shed light on how to provide followers with the proof points they need to judge potential leaders against the values dimension. That is why the story is worth exploring further.

First delivered in his 2004 Democratic National Convention keynote address, and borrowed from his former pastor Jeremiah Wright (a loan that would come back to haunt him during his first presidential election campaign), the phrase 'the audacity of hope' captured the mood of America (and that of many of us soft intellectual, bleeding-heart, left-leaning liberals, as our friends across the Atlantic like to think of us, without exception, who happen to live this side of the pond!)

2006 was one of those turning-point years. In the first half of the first decade of a new millennium, happiness had been the norm, not hope. Credit was easy. Life was sweet. But the prosperity experienced by most was built on unprecedented levels of debt. Mortgages categorized as sub-prime (a term few were familiar with) had risen from a low 8 per cent of the mortgage stock to an all-time high of 20 per cent. The ratio of debt to disposable income had gone from 77 per cent in the 1990s to a record breaking 127 per cent in 2007. Comatose but happy, like a drunk postponing a hangover by never stopping drinking, we had a relentless thirst for possessions and the availability of credit was bottomless.

2006 was the beginning of the wake-up call that no amount of snooze-button pushing would be able to delay. House prices reached their peak and started, at first a slow, then a relentless, decline akin to that experienced on the Disney rides families visited on their credit-fuelled lifestyles. Indebted and unable to meet the now rising variable rates they had signed for (with or without full understanding as it happens), households started to default on their mortgage debt as never before. Almost a quarter of US homes became worth less than the mortgages secured against them. Foreclosures increased to previously unseen levels.

The magic financial products created by millionaire quants[1] in cities as distant from each other as New York, London, Singapore or Hong Kong lost their shine. As triple-A products became junk investments, a wave of unease started to take hold. Chased by an ever rising number of foreclosures, individuals realized that what they had lived through hadn't been prosperity but conjuring. And, just as the rabbits magicians pull out of hats have to be put in there in the first place, we now realized that banks couldn't create money. The money coming out of the hat was running out, and outside the hat no one was producing it.

Unable to evaluate the now worthless amounts of mortgage-backed securities they held, financial firms and global investors reduced their exposures. Inter-bank lending, the blood in the financial system's veins, stopped flowing. Economic growth all but disappeared. The final scene of this first act of our global depression came on 15 September 2008 when the fourth-largest American investment bank declared bankruptcy, filing for Chapter 11. The image of Lehman employees filing out of the bank's headquarters with their cardboard boxes, in the same way their clients had filed out with their cash and investors with their investments, imprinted itself on our collective psyche as a summary of our excesses.

In a relatively short two years from the publication of *The Audacity of Hope* to the presidential election, hope had gone from unnecessary (why hope when everything looks fine) to almost inappropriate (in doom we find it hard to differentiate hope from mindless optimism). As economists stopped contradicting each other to admit they just didn't know and pundits preached the end of the world as we knew it, answers were hard to find and despair set in.

It took more than a book to rebuild the otherwise unflinching American spirit, and it would be foolish to argue that the book or indeed the president stood as the proverbial American cavalry saving the day in the best tradition of western spaghetti movies. Yet *The Audacity of Hope* became the rallying cry of a movement for change. The attraction of that movement is irrefutable (it elected a president). It is that attraction, rather than its politics, that is of interest here.

It would be easy to suggest that rousing speeches and oratory skills alone can turn the tide of despair. It would be easy to suggest that a well-crafted vision or a dream can achieve a reversal of fortune. After all another African-American leader, the Reverend Martin Luther King, had proved that having a dream could mobilize a nation. But dreaming alone doesn't change anything. Dreaming is the preserve of the sleeper and whilst sleepers may move about they seldom walk forward.

In fact, even though it was famous, Martin Luther King's dream did not achieve much on its own. Having had his dream, Martin Luther King woke up and walked up. As he told the assembled crowd in the Mason Temple, headquarters of the Church of God in Christ, Memphis, Tennessee, he had been to the mountaintop and seen the other side. You only have to read a transcript from the speech to realize that Martin Luther King was no dreamer. The Reverend had a plan. The speech outlined practical steps for followers and exhorted them for when times would inevitably be hard. Reverend King did have a dream but he also had a goal, a will and a way. Reverend King generated hope not dreams. And so too did the senator from Illinois.

Whilst Senator Obama's 2006 book and 2008 campaign for the United States of America's presidency brought hope to the foreground in an otherwise gloomy and frightened world, it is fair to say that the concept of hope and its application to leadership had been looked at for some time before the downturn. Countless research papers, experiments and studies have shown how hope is linked to happiness, motivation, the evasion of destructive emotions and all round well-being in our lives. Despite this ever expanding body of work the concept of hope is still hard to define. Is it the same as the optimism so many self-help books exhort us to adopt? Is it the same as dreams or beliefs? Is it the preserve of great ambitions or does it exist in small wishes?

In his book, the then Senator Obama might well have written about 'the audacity of hope' but in so doing he offered us a great case study in the anatomy of hope (Figure 5.1). Etymologically the word hope contains the ideas of both wish and expectation. It is that concept of expectation that differentiates hope from dreams and beliefs. In another book about hope, *The Psychology of Hope*, CR Snyder defines it as 'the sum of the mental willpower and way-power that you have for your goal'. It is that sum that Reverend King and Senator Obama managed to compute.

The Audacity of Hope outlines a goal – the reclaiming of the American dream. By walking through the struggles of the author as well as pointing to the struggles ahead, the book encourages readers to remember that the American dream is all about the will to succeed. Never give up. If you want it enough you can succeed. The very slogan of the movement – 'yes we can' – repeated endlessly at rallies up and down the country, is the cry of willpower. As in the all-American story of the little engine that could, by repeating yes we can, rally delegates were doing as much to convince themselves as to convince those around them. Willpower is the sum total of the times 'yes we can' is repeated. Finally, described by *The New York Times* as 'a political document' that reads like a 'stump speech' and is 'devoted to laying out Mr Obama's policy positions on a host of issues from education to health care to the war in Iraq', the book offers a plan on how to reach that goal.[2] That plan gave the movement the waypower that Snyder shows us is necessary for hope.

Figure 5.1 The anatomy of hope

From the time of his announcement on a cold day in Springfield, Illinois, on 10 February 2007 until 27 August 2008 when he was nominated, Senator Barack Obama had pinned his colours to one mast – that of hope. It was hope that took the Junior United States Senator to the Democratic Party nomination for the 2008 presidential election almost a month to the day before Lehman's Chapter 11 filing. It was hope that would repay him less than three months later when, on 4 November 2008, he was elected the first African-American president of the United States of America.

For the sake of political balance and to underscore the fact that in no way is the beginning of this chapter an advert in disguise for a set of political ideas (propaganda being something *Fox News* is keen to accuse President Obama of), allow me a few seconds of detour.

The origin of the modern Tea Party movement is complex and disputed. Whether you like to think that it emerged out of the failed libertarian 2008 election campaign of Congressman Ron Paul or take the view that Trevor Leach the Chairman of the Young Americans for Liberty in New York State started it all with a gathering, or even if you're an advocate of the Koch brothers' industrialists and activists, you are unlikely to disagree that it was on 19 February 2009, on the floor of the Chicago Mercantile Exchange, that the movement took hold.

In a now well-publicized, YouTube sensationalized intervention, CNBC *Business News*' Rick Santelli demonized a government that had, the day before, proposed a plan for the refinancing of mortgages (losers' loans as Santelli famously described them). Santelli's rant, supplemented by traders on the floor, oblivious to their role in the downturn, had the desired effect.[3] The following day *Fox News* started to refer to the Tea Party movement. It took Santelli's views to be turned into a plan by Ryan Hecker and his 'Contract from America' to give supporters the encouragement and the way they were looking for. By 2010 the Tea Party's views and a broader realignment behind a free-market agenda had such an impact on the election cycle that the new-found Republican hope took over the reins of Congress.

I am in no way being facetious when I say that the Tea Party movement and President Obama have a lot more in common than either would ever agree to! In a review of *The Audacity of Hope*, the *Chicago Tribune* describes it as 'a political biography that concentrates on the senator's core values'.[4] The Tea Party movement, despite its many faces and self-managing branches, unites under the flag of free-market values. Both have a goal, a will and a way.

This is why I felt it appropriate, politics aside, to open this chapter with a focus on *The Audacity of Hope*. No story could better fit the values dimension. In his book, President Obama was laying down the markers that would help followers answer the second part of the first question of leadership – 'Does the potential leader share my values?' Compassion alone does not answer the values dimension. Compassion shows care, but it is hope that demonstrates an alignment of values.

In that way American politics is no different from any other field of human endeavour anywhere in the world. The first step to becoming a leader is to generate hope through compassion. 'I hear you', 'understand you', 'feel what you feel', 'value what you value' but 'I can also see a way forward': these are the words we look for in our potential leaders. These words are the words of compassion and hope. And they are words that we, business people, too often glance over.

The examples I chose to open this chapter with, from Martin Luther King to the Tea Party Movement via Obama, are useful reminders of how hope works. Using hope does require an understanding of the three elements – goal, way and will. The examples are however potentially misleading.

All three examples relate to times of struggle. And at times of hardship it is easy to see what the goal might be – get out of the struggle. It is also easy to understand how followers will be willing to follow. After all it seems that it is at times of trouble that we tend to follow the most toxic leaders and their oversimplified recipe for change (human history is peppered with conflicts started in times of crisis). What a crisis situation does is make the crowd more responsive to the leader. In crisis we want even more reassurance so we look for leaders.

But let's face it, despite what we might like to tell our children or would like our partners to believe, for many of us, we do not operate in these types of struggle in everyday life. Building, marketing, selling or trading stuff is hardly the thing great movies are made off (unless you include cheating, deceiving or killing as part of your duties). When business is tough (which it always is) rather than desperate, we feel the need to get on but seldom do we stop and think about the need for hope.

Leaders are often quick to describe events as crises as a way to establish themselves and their agenda as the only hope. This may well be why so many of them spend so much time trying to create a sense of urgency via 'a burning platform'. I have always found the analogy of a burning platform somewhat repulsive. Call it my networks of association, but for anyone who is remotely connected to the oil industry the images that the analogy conjures are deeply disturbing. I will come back at length to the use of analogies as tools of leadership but I fear that, even discounting my personal feelings for this one, it is one of the most dangerous analogies one can use in business. Not only is it sick and repulsive but it is also wrong.

People on burning platforms do not orderly align themselves to a goal. They react in three ways – the most primitive ways known to man. They either fight or they fly. Or they remain static, frozen (a poor yet unavoidable choice of word) in place by fear. One thing is for sure though: people on burning platforms are not talked into a crisis – they can feel it. I am sure many of you, like me, have stood in a hotel room or meeting while the fire alarm sounded, wondering if it really warranted your leaving the warmth of your bed or the brilliantly engrossing meeting (ok maybe the meeting is a bad example). The alarm that sounded for the financial crisis wasn't something people were just reading about or listening to. It was something people felt.

This is why I started this rundown through the elements of emotional logic with compassion. Compassion is critical to the values dimension in so far as it helps us articulate hope. Leaders do not impose their hopes and dreams on others. Leaders amplify the goals of their followers and turn them into hope through will and way, not engineered fear mongering, so-called 'burning platforms'.

Stage 1: articulate the goal

So our starting point must be to remember that, to make a valid assessment of the values dimension, followers look not only for proof that the potential leader cares about them (which compassion is an indicator of) but also for proof of alignment between their values and those they perceive the potential leader to have. The proof point for that alignment is the articulated goal of the leader. As we saw earlier hope can only be present when a goal is articulated. If there is no goal there can be no hope as there is nothing to hope for. So as strange as it may seem, it is the goal that is the first step to hope.

Of course, a lot has been written about goals in business, usually articulated on a spectrum from a long-range vision to targeted SMART (Specific, Measurable, Achievable, Realistic and Time-bound) objectives, with plans sitting somewhere in the middle. Before you rush off to polish your vision statements or dig out the job description buried deep in the bottom drawer of your desk to sharpen these, let me point out that this is not where the value of goals in hope lies.

The articulation of a goal in hope is a dialogue, not a monologue. Others have written at length about the need for a leader to have hope to be effective. But to ignite emotional logic, leaders must ensure that the hope is shared. The goal must be sufficiently personal to the leader to be believed, but sufficiently shared to be generative. It isn't enough for leaders to articulate their hope, even if this is done masterfully and vividly. It isn't enough for followers to see the goal as theirs – they must own it as such.

On the other hand leaders must add value. They, too, must share in the goal. To stay in the realm of politics, leaders are often accused of 'leading by focus groups' or 'flip-flopping on issues depending on where the electorate goes'. Effective leaders lead. They do not ask and flip-flop. For sure they listen and change their minds but that is a different dynamic – one where the leader has a position and a view. Whether in a crisis or not, people look for leaders not mirrors. As I mentioned in the introduction, role-based leadership is a game of inclusion (people have to follow you so you need to engage them) whereas real leadership is a game of exclusion and polarization (followers need to make a choice between alternatives). The goal is what ensures the right people make that choice and follow.

So how do you create your goal and yet align it to followers' expectations? Over the last few years I have been lucky enough to work with Clare Sheikh as she took on numerous roles in the world of brands. From ITV to Vodafone via RSA I have witnessed her and her team extract the core purpose of an organization. Being able to take a narrative down to its essential core goal and engage an organization around it is what Clare does best. When working at the UK's Automobile Association she coined the term 'Britain's fourth emergency service' for the road recovery service. At ITV, at a time when everyone thought the future of TV would be small digital channels watched in isolation, she gave them 'TV to talk about' before what broadcasting professionals now call 'event TV' had even registered on their radars. To help her in that work she uses a very simple model originally developed by advertising supremos Maurice and Charles Saatchi. She calls it the three-box model (Figure 5.2). Here is how it works.

Figure 5.2   The three-box model to purpose building

In the first box goes something that is true about the world. That is added to a truth about you to give us the brand essence. Of course, the truth about the world is not easily reached, hence the need for compassion. Without compassion or hope, leaders are unable to understand the truth about the people they aim to attract. The truth about the self however is even harder to gain. We like to think we are many things, but in this case whatever we think we offer is of no importance. What really matters is what can be substantiated.

A good example Clare gives is the work done by GSK pharmaceutical. The truth about the world is that people are afraid of diseases. That seems true enough; we are all afraid of getting something bad. The truth about GSK is that their R&D spend is higher that of its competitors. Again this can easily be substantiated. The resulting core purpose is: 'We are disease's biggest enemy.'

Now imagine you work for a pharmaceutical. What would you rather do – produce some pills and tablets or slay some viruses? What is more likely to drive you as a noble purpose? But more importantly, which is more likely to help you make decisions and move forward in your role? Being disease's biggest enemy creates a simple goal that helps you work out what the future may hold.

As you can see from the image above I have changed the organizational domain to a personal one. Be it the 'Yes we can' of the Obama 2008 campaign or the 'Making a dint in the Universe' of Steve Jobs, pithy mantras don't only offer the tag line to a product but rather contain the essence of the direction the leader intends to travel in. The key is not to focus on the tag line but to work to inform the two critical truths of the three-box model. Trying to find a tag line is not easy, but it is also empty unless it rests in two truths. It is the validity of those truths that makes the difference between the tag line living on a poster or in the minds of our followers informing their actions.

Step 1: find your truth

Unlike the three-box model, I propose you start with you, rather than followers.

When we think about goals we tend to think about narrow objectives (raise sales by …) or grand outcomes (to govern as the president). Whilst both these are legitimate they never tap into the real drivers of your desire to lead. The truth is often to be found in the why.

Ask yourself why you want to lead. Why you? Goffee and Jones of London Business School said it best in the title of their best-selling book, *Why Should Anyone Be Led by You?*[5] Why should anyone be led by you is indeed a difficult question to answer. I have been playing around with this idea with aspiring leaders for some time and what struck me most is how little time we spend thinking about leadership.

In today's organization, leadership is the logical outcome of promotion. It is viewed as the pinnacle of a career. The more successful we are, the bigger the team and scope we get. The assumption many make is that leadership is the logical outcome of success. But why? What are you trying to prove and to whom? These are not trivial questions as they underpin your motivation and therefore ultimately your goal. Few of us are courageous enough to ask what truly drives us, fearing the answer might be nothing. What if we have no goal or no dream? The reality is that we all live in a psychological world of 'shoulds' inherited from our upbringing or the expectations we feel are placed on us by our social environments. 'Shoulds' are not goals until they are replaced by 'wants' derived through a process of introspection. It is the building of that self-awareness that is the starting point of leadership. Without a personal goal there can be no leading others.

Most choose to answer these questions in the same way as they produce a CV or prepare for a job interview by listing a series of 'whats': 'I am good at bringing people around to a goal, I am good at motivating others, I have a great sense of humour and a passion for hard work, I have high standards, I have been told I have authority.' Yet, leaders become so through who they are, not just what they can or can't do. The questions that help develop self-awareness are a mixture of why and what questions. Why do you want to lead? Who are you trying to please and why? What are you seeking and why? They are not the questions others ask, they are the questions you should ask of yourself.

Only when you identify what drives your desire to lead can you articulate your value as a leader. Only when you know your dream will you be able to start articulating the value question that underpins your truth. What is the value that you offer as a leader that no one else can offer more effectively or efficiently? Remember that the three-box model above calls for a truth that is not only believable but demonstrable. You must find your proof points. What in your experience and personal history justified your assertion of your value?

Step 2: identify followers' truth

As I pointed out earlier it is a mistake to assume that you must understand everyone and appeal to them. The people you must truly understand are the people you can identify as your constituency. Who are the followers you need? Who would you identify as the great followers who appear in the subtitle of this book. Obedient followers are for leaders who don't stand for anything. Leaders understand the needs of the followers who share in their dreams. In our GSK example above the followers' truth resided in their view of illness and medicine because that is the field GSK plays in.

How would you characterize the followers you need? I am guessing not as people who have special identifiable personal characteristics (I need people who are not afraid of change and know something about accountancy), but rather as people who share in your goal (I need followers who are driven by the idea of defying the status quo in the PC industry). When you are able to articulate the field of play you can then use all the three building blocks of compassion we saw in the previous chapter to understand the underpinning truth of that constituency. What is it that unites them? What is the one thing they dream of? How would they articulate the information you gain through compassion?

Step 3: articulate the goal

Having a dream and identifying the dreams of your potential constituency is the first step, but knowing how to articulate it for resonance is key. It is the articulation of the goal that we remember. From 'I have a dream' to 'We will fight them on the beaches' it is words that carry us. We will come back in Chapter 7 to the importance of rhetoric in creating the resonance that leads to charisma.

At this stage however you should not be thinking so much about the articulation of the catchy one-liner but rather about how you envisage the goal. This is Box Three. How do you put one and two together? What is it in the value you offer that will resonate with your constituency?

Our goals are likely, first, to take the form of a list of alternatives and wishes applied to a number of domains (these are the things that are desirable in our lives, our work, our family relationships etc). To spotlight the way is to devise a plan. For this to happen, short and long-range goals must be prioritized. It is in that prioritization step that plans usually surface. The process of prioritization will generate further details on the meaning of the goals and the process of goal achievement. It is therefore important that this step is done on paper rather than just as a thought process, as alternatives and connections will become too numerous to be remembered.

The key to goal setting is focus. By highlighting what gets in the way of you articulating your goals you are likely to identify the barriers to their fulfilment. The articulation of the goal comes to life through a leader's ability to nurture followers' will and spotlight the way for them.

Stage 2: nurture willpower and spotlight the way

The issue of willpower is one that has fascinated business writers for some time, not to say philosophers and thinkers for centuries. How to ensure you have the will to carry on is a question many have been pondering. Willpower, like goals, doesn't have to be directed to times of crisis; it is part of the human condition from the time we get up in the morning (itself requiring willpower) to the time we put the lights out. The question here however is not just how leaders ensure they have the will to lead but also, and more importantly, how you ensure others have the willpower to follow. There are three areas of focus for leaders aiming to ensure their followers find the strength to fulfil the goal.

Step 1: feed self-talk

The mantra 'Yes we can' of the Obama campaign wasn't chosen by chance (not much is ever left to chance in any campaign). The biggest obstacle to goal achievement is our self-talk – that little voice in our heads that tell us we can't. External barriers pale in comparison to self-talk. By choosing the 'Yes we can' mantra, the Obama campaign was working to nurture a new self-talk. 'Yes we can' is as clear a self-talk replacement strategy as you'll ever get but it's now been taken and you would come across pretty poorly if you were to borrow it, so the question is: What is your mantra?

Ensuring the right self-talk is in place is not just about focusing on a mantra followers recall during the goal achievement process; it is also about focusing their discussions on positive outcomes. I will come back in the last part of this book to what is called, somewhat pedantically I guess, appreciative inquiry – a process of focusing conversations on positive desirable outcomes. However at this stage it is important that that the goal is crafted in language of what I want and what I choose. The job of the leader in hope is to frame the conversations in a way that reiterates the desirability of the goal for followers not just for the leaders. How often do you remind followers of what they have chosen rather than what you desire?

Inevitably there will be barriers in the achievement of the goal and these will seriously question the will of all involved. There are two ways to ensure followers retain hope by retaining their will. The first is to recall past successes.

We take comfort from knowing that we have passed tests previously when we are faced with a new one. Do you have a bank of stories of when success was achieved in testing times and barriers overcome? These should not only be stories about you (although your personal resilience matters), but more broadly stories about collective achievement.

The second is to never underestimate the power of humour. Laughing in the face of adversity is a great way to defuse the early onset of despair. I will not go as far as using the well-known line of the old *Readers' Digest* – laughter is the best medicine – as I do think that drugs have a great part to play in cures. There is however power in using humour to re-humanize a situation that may feel as though it requires superhuman strengths.

Of course, there will come a time when the barriers faced in the achievement of a goal are not just internal barriers to followers and leaders. Sometimes, the barriers will be external and very real. This is where waypower becomes critical. Whilst the expression 'where there is a will, there is a way' might well be true, our innate need to follow suggests that we are attracted to leaders who propose a way for us. That is not to say that we blindly follow, but rather that we find strength in knowing that others share our goals and project a strength to achieve them that we find reassuring. Giving waypower to followers does not mean having a fully worked out strategy. Waypower is about highlighting the path and what travelling it will entail.

Step 2: signpost the route

I mentioned earlier on that when crafting your goal you are likely to have designed a number of sub-goals. Treat these as the signposts on the road to achievement. As we will see later, sub-goals play an important part in the measurement element of the achievement dimension. Even adventurous travellers have a road map. It doesn't have to detailed but it needs to indicate some of the main landmarks and turning points. Signposting the route reassures us that there is a way. What are the main landmarks you will visit on the road to goal achievement?

Not all barriers will be as easy to avoid as the famously failed Maginot line, the large edifice the French built on their coast to stop the German advance during the Second World War, which the Germans decided to just go around! Some barriers will stand strong even in the face of the strongest will. In this case what are your escape routes? What are the alternative routes that can be jumped on to continue your way?

You need to be clear on what role you and your followers will play on the road and the review points when you may simply need to review your route or indeed revise your goal. I have been lucky to work alongside the McLaren Formula 1 team in my consulting practice and I am always amazed at how much planning goes into what can go wrong. For all these barriers, plans are made and pit-stop strategies prepared so that setbacks are only perceived as normal occurrences on the way to success. Unlike what you may hear motivational speakers say, you may not be the best, the strongest, wisest, fittest or any other 'est' you care to mention, but you can always be the best prepared. That is always within your control. So you must be clear about your 'pit-stops' strategy.

Step 3: use the force

I have always been wary of the singular relentless focus on strengths that seems to have taken hold in organizations. I am painfully too aware that what derails many executive careers are weaknesses that go unchecked and as a result become amplified.

However, if we focus on our weaknesses, hope becomes a rather ephemeral concept. Success in creating hope is achieved when we understand the nature of our strengths and how they enable us to navigate the tortuous path. For leaders this shouldn't mean denying weaknesses, but rather ensuring that strengths are highlighted for each step of the way. This necessitates constant dialogue with followers around the question of what our common skills are that will ensure our success.

There is one concept I have only slightly touched upon in this chapter that yet underscores most of its value. That is the concept of choice. We can only truly hope when we have made the choice of the goal, have chosen to exercise our willpower and are working towards this. Choice however is not something management and leadership theorists spend a lot of time writing about. After all, seldom do we choose our leaders in business, at least once we have chosen to invest our effort in one particular company. Whilst we have fought hard for democracy in our countries and free markets in our econo-mies, these very same ideas have found it hard to penetrate the thick walls of our corporations. Yet, of course, choice is the very essence of this book – leaders are such because we, as followers, choose to make them so.

We choose to follow some leaders over others. Making a choice assumes that differentiation exists. If two things are the same you may take one over the other. Whilst we may call this 'choosing one' as a shorthand, 'picking' is not the same as the act of 'being drawn' that followership infers. Followership requires alternatives, and alternatives are such because they have identifiable characteristics that polarize. It is these characteristics followers look for when they undertake the character dimension of emotional logic in their search for the answer to the question 'Do these people have what it takes to do right by my values and represent my interest?'

It is these characteristics we now must move to.

The tweet

Hope gives impetus to followership by highlighting a desired state (goal), that can be reached (will) through a series of steps (way).

Notes

1 'Quant' is a term used on Wall Street to designate the experts in quantitative finance who used their expertise in advanced mathematics to build complex financial products.

2 Kakutani, M (2006) 'Obama's foursquare politics, with a dab of Dijon', *New York Times*, 17 October.

3 Ok I did say I would avoid becoming political or one sided but I have to admit that I have never been a fan of any crowd of angry young men (they were mostly men) regardless of their affiliation, so forgive me for my unsympathetic tone.

4 Dorning, M (2006) 'First glimpse of Obama's new memoir', 6 Oct 2006, *Chicago Tribune*, 5 October.

5 Goffee, R and Jones, G (2006) *Why Should Anyone be Led by You?*, Harvard Business School Press.

PART THREE
THE CHARACTER DIMENSION

Having looked at how leaders can start to connect to potential followers through the values dimension, it is now time to turn to the second element of emotional logic – the character dimension.

In the character dimension, potential followers are looking for affirmation that the leader will be able to act in line with those values. They are looking to see if the leader offers a viable choice as the person best suited to enact a vision. They are asking themselves – does that person have what it takes to make decisions based on my values? Will they be tough enough and have enough integrity to stay true even when times get tough?

There are four elements that underpin decision making at play in the character dimension – asperity, rhetoric, integrity and simplicity. We will look at each of these in turn as we continue to spell out charisma.

The character dimension of emotional logic

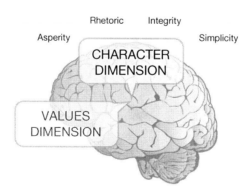

CHAPTER 6
ASPERITY

Underpinning question and why it matters

What is asperity and why does it matter to followers?

In physics, asperity is defined as the unevenness of a surface. Even the most polished of surfaces are rough at an atomic scale. So it is for leaders. In the character dimension followers look for the right mix of smooth and rough. We want our leaders' visions and hopes to be well articulated but we also want them to be rough in the defence of that vision. We want them to be better than us yet share our flaws.

Maybe she was really born in Berne, Switzerland, in 1760 as she claimed or maybe she was actually born in Strasbourg, France, as the registry records show. Maybe her mother did take her to church to be baptized as she fondly recalled, or maybe, as the parish records suggest, it was the local midwife who took her there. Maybe her father, Joseph Grosholtz, a decorated soldier, missed her birth having recently passed away, but we'll have to take her word for it as no records exist of the man.

Maybe her stories are designed to deceive or maybe they are there to engage. Maybe it is the historical truth that matters or maybe the well-crafted myth is fine. You will have to decide for yourself, based on the intent you ascribe to her and the values you create for yourself. But one thing is certain. One thing is beyond doubt or judgement. As she entered this world, no one could have foreseen what Anna Maria Grosholtz would become.

Despite decades of progress and hard-fought struggles for equality, a woman entrepreneur, company director, marketing genius with global name recognition is still only too rare today, but in the turbulent world of 18th-century Europe it was even more of a feat. It was a feat she fought so hard to accomplish that her name still resonates in our collective psyche some 250 years later. That name and her two children are all she got from her marriage to a man who would consume more than he contributed to their union. That name is Tussaud, Anna Maria Tussaud. A name known to us all in solid shiny yellow letters on a red background above the doors of entertainment venues throughout the world as Madame Tussauds.[1]

Anna Maria learnt her trade at the side of Dr Philippe Curtius. The physician from Berne, Switzerland, took a liking for his housekeeper's daughter and decided to teach her everything he knew. Mysteries abound as to the nature of the relationship between Curtius and Anna Maria's mother. Whatever the truth, the, at times, mentor, business partner, uncle and surrogate father, became the most influential person in her life.

She was only 15 when she created her first wax figure and for 30 odd years following Dr Curtius's death in 1794, Anna Maria travelled Europe exhibiting her numerous works to the enchantment of the crowds who flocked to see them. As well as a trade, he gave Anna Maria the perseverance, grit, single mindedness and the knack for celebrity branding that we need to move on to as we reach the first step of the achievement dimension and our third element of charisma.

There is one key issue with the values dimension we encountered in the last two chapters – the answers can be faked. It is possible to look like you care or project a message of hope you do not believe in. Experiments in care homes and hospitals show how animals or robots can help people who are lonely by providing what looks like compassion and hope. Philosophers might want to argue that what is seen, experienced and believed to be compassion and hope is indeed compassion and hope, but the reality of human interactions indicates otherwise.

What offers relief in those contexts also carries the risk of diminishing the interaction over time: the patient comes to realize that the relief provided by an animal or robot is useful but is no replacement for the deeper connections of a human-to-human experience. Even if we can be fooled some of the time, unless we decide to ignore them (and we often try to), we detect fissures between the actor and his/her personality. We come to believe that the projected image differs from the shaded reality. Our subconscious brain detects inconsistencies before our conscious thoughts are ready to accept them. This is why, when emotional logic helps us decide on who we follow, it doesn't only rely on values but looks for another dimension. I call this search the character dimension.

Whilst followers look for shared values they also assess the leadership potential of an individual by trying to understand if that person will uphold those values when making decisions. Whilst followers look for a compassionate leader with a message of hope they also look for a leader with a knowledge of reality and the character to face up to its challenges. A leader's single mindedness to confront real challenges matters. A leader's ability to articulate clearly a path to success matters. Leaders who do what they say, and say what they think, are ones who matter. Leaders who remove complexity matter. Asperity, rhetoric, integrity and simplicity are the defining characteristics of the character dimension.

When we choose leaders we want to know if they are the real deal or well-trained fakes. Are they the genuine article or wax models? Madame Tussaud would know all about the difference – and as such, through both her life and her work, has something to teach us.

The starting point of our journey through the character dimension is asperity. In physics asperity is defined as the unevenness of a surface. Every surface is rough. Even the most polished of surfaces are rough at an atomic scale. Glass may feel smooth but a microscope will reveal the hidden mountainous landscape the eye never sees and the fingers never feel. When it comes to emotional logic, our brain acts as the microscope. It gauges asperity. It assesses the smoothness and the roughness of a leader. It looks for the crack in the patina.

In material science, understanding asperity is critical. When surfaces rub against one another, it is first the points of roughness that collide and determine the strength of a material. The analogy can be carried through to leadership. We look for our leaders to have a certain amount of grit to measure their strength. There are two determinants of strength. One is grit of character.

Does the person we look to lead us have enough self-determination to make things happen? The other is granularity of work. Is the person we look to lead us close enough to the everyday reality of life to turn ideas and strategies into actions? Asperity defines both Anna Maria Tussaud and her work.

Stage 1: grit of character

What is fascinating about the history of waxworks is their enduring appeal. It is easy to see why in Madam Tussaud's times they would have resonated. News travelled by word of mouth and seldom was it seen. The rulers lived in palaces removed from the reality and the gaze of the populace. The fashion of the day and the excesses of the few fascinated as they do today, the difference being that, for most people, they remained an unseen dream.

It is that dream world that Madame Tussaud and the countless other wax artists of the time brought to life. They didn't talk about wax museums preserving the past; theirs were three-dimensional newspapers. They were depictions of the lives others lived. Waxworks were the TV screens of the day – tableaux assembled to describe the unseen scenes the other half (although far smaller than a half) lived.

But given that we now have 24-hour access to the celebrities of today, why does the fascination endure? The answer can be found in the winding line of visitors to Madame Tussauds on Marylebone Road, London. The promise of showing us the world of the famous is no longer one the waxworks can claim. We know more about how our celebrities live than even they seem to. We know what the famous look like, what they sound like, how they dress and how they live and, if the multitude of celebrity perfumes are to be believed, we even know what they smell like. The only thing that remains ephemeral is proximity and that is what people will wait patiently in line to experience.

We have seen, heard and smelled them, but we still haven't touched them. So, in keeping with the promise of bringing us closer to the famous, Merlin Entertainment (the company that manages Madame Tussauds' assets) has once again evolved. Through the magic of wax, those who can be called superior to us by class or fame are now at our level. The ropes that kept visitors at bay, as observers of their own times have come down. In the final evolution of the waxwork genre, you can now be part of the world into which Madame Tussaud herself only gave you a glimpse.

I am sure there are a lot of studies to be found, for those who care enough, that explain our fascination with the famous and our desire to be photographed next to their wax effigies. And whilst interesting, this is of little concern to me here. What I am interested in is why Madame Tussaud herself became famous. What set her apart from others? The answer: grit of character.

We have all mastered the art of 'talking business'. We have learnt the buzz-words that will get us by in a game of business bingo. We know the right noises to make and the right efficiency buttons to push to sound like a leader. We know what to say and how to say it so well that we might easily forget why we are saying it. But what happens when the going gets tough? What happens when smooth is no longer enough? What Anna Maria Grosholtz displayed and Madame Tussaud turned into an art form was strength of character and resilience that endured the toughest of challenges. She showed a level of self-belief and determination seldom seen in leaders.

That self-belief and determination gave her resilience in the face of obstacles. The association of belief in her purpose with belief in herself is what asperity is about. The ability never to deviate from the core is what grit of character is. Under the character dimension, followers try to ascertain if the potential leader has what it takes to uphold those values, when faced with the reality of leading. Being able to stand true in face of that reality is what Madame Tussaud did. As regimes and markets changed around her and her economic circum-stances became worse, it would have been easy for her to abandon or change her business but she didn't. There are two steps that enabled her to withstand the relentless onslaught of reality.

Step 1: know what you stand for

Something strange happens to anyone studying or joining a business. We all become 'business smooth'. Our desire for recognition from our superiors and peers in corporate hierarchies, or for results in business schools, makes us change. We learn the language in order to fit. We learn what is acceptable and what isn't – the way we do things around here – the culture of the organization and the culture of work. Yet that longing to belong can blind us to our own views. We feel that to be accepted, let alone promoted, we need to fit the mould and bend to the rules of an imaginary game.

I am always surprised at the willingness of young executives to disregard what they think in favour of what they think others expect them to think. That desire to bend to the rules rather than bend them is the direct result of our desire to fit. Yet there is a strange paradox in leadership. Whilst to climb the corporate ladder we feel we need to curtail our opinions, it is these very opinions that actually differentiate us. We convince ourselves that to be noticed we need to be unnoticeable. We aim to be normal (ie average) in order to be differentiated. We become character chameleons. And whilst adaptability and a healthy dose of emotional intelligence are necessary to protect us from alienation, only by remaining true to who we are can we ever be successful.

Followers do not want 'business smooth'. Their context is 'business rough'. Followers demand leadership not because they expect leaders to make the uncertain certain, but because they take courage from knowing that even in an uncertain world a path can be followed. So the leadership paradox is that whilst we may want our leaders to have mastered 'business smooth' and talk a good game not to be ostracised, we also need to see them performing in 'business rough' to be successful.

One of the things Madame Tussaud possessed was certainty of what she stood for. For all of her career she knew that what set her apart was her gift for storytelling and entrepreneurship. She would not sacrifice her desire to succeed with shortcuts to appeal to the fashions of the day. At a time when exhibitions were put on that would appeal to the lowest common denominator (ie soft pornography), titillating the masses and bringing in short-term revenue, she continued to make high-quality tableaux of the news of the day in the knowledge that hers was a sustainable business.

Does that mean you are never receptive to the needs of others? Does it mean you never deviate from a course of action? Of course not – remember, the model is not cyclical or linear. Compassion and hope force you to be receptive to the needs of others. But if you become others, you have nothing to offer them. Grit of character means that you know what you stand for and the value you bring.

So where do you start? My recommendation would be to make two lists. One is the list of what you stand for (eg security, innovation, new ideas, calm, certainty of process…) Whatever that list contains that is dear to you are the 'non-negotiable' items. These are the things that define you. The other list should be of the things that you will not do (eg go for short-term value to the detriment of long-term relationships, compromise on quality of output…). This list gives you the boundaries for your flexibility. It tells you where the rough will hit the smooth. It ensures that you know the battles you will fight. Of course lists are pretty useless unless they are enacted and this is where Step 2 comes in.

Step 2: be resilient in the face of change

Being ruthless in terms of what you believe and having a no-compromise attitude for the things that are important is hard for human beings, as we fear rejection from others. Compromise however erodes delivery – every time we compromise we may not take anything away from the vision but we delay its delivery. Character is best defined as the choices we make, and the choices we make are what defines our leadership impact. Emotional logic does not respond well to average (which is also why we can be so attracted to leaders who are ultimately flawed). So even when things change, we need to be prepared to be resilient and stick to our vision.

In 1803, things had taken a turn for the worse for Madame Tussaud. She was travelling around Scotland and Ireland, having forged a poor business partnership with a showman intent on using her to subsidize his failing show. Knowing the situation was unsustainable, Anna Maria worked hard to repay her debt and free herself. She knew she could succeed only if she stuck to what she did. In fact she did stick to her vision and did succeed – but not without sacrifice.

Her husband, a lazy profligate, wanted her back in Paris where he was making a poor job of looking after one of their children. In a extraordinarily poignant letter that revealed much of her character, Madame Tussaud told him in no uncertain terms 'I am not ready to return yet. I will not return without a well-filled purse.' Not only did this letter indicate the poor state of the marriage but also the fact that, despite the challenges she was encountering and the loneliness she must have felt, separated from one of her children, Anna Maria Tussaud would go on.

Having decided what you stand for (the value you bring and the vision you hold) along with the things about which you will not compromise on (the non-negotiable), it is now time to make a third list. This list is possibly the hardest and most personal list you will have to make, but it is also the best predictor of your ability to meet the challenge of asperity. This is a list of the things you are prepared to sacrifice. Leadership is not easy and true leadership requires sacrifice. When people talk about the passion to lead, I tend to see the word passion more in the context of the Passion of Christ, rather than passion as joy. Leadership requires sacrifice, and without identifying this first it is impossible for us to know if we can ever succeed.

The key to success is to be strong enough to fulfil our purpose whilst remaining flexible enough to do so, given the constraints of the reality we work under. For this to be possible, grit of character needs to be associated with an understanding of the environment within which we operate. This understanding is what I call 'granularity of work'.

Stage 2: granularity of work

As well as being the embodiment of grit of character, Madame Tussaud displays, through her work, the second dimension of asperity I call granularity of work. Have you ever wondered why we all seem so desperate to know whether our presidents or prime ministers know the price of a loaf of bread or a carton of milk? Asperity is the answer – I need to know if they know the price of milk because I need to know if they will be able to make decisions in line with my values in the real world. I know they talk a good game (that's the values dimension) but can they also play one. Do they know their stuff at a level of granularity that is sufficient for them to make the tough calls.

The idea contained behind what I call 'granularity of work' was best summarized by one of my consulting clients in the brewing industry who once lamented after a particularly slide-heavy presentation on a supply chain by a well-known strategy house: 'The problem with those people is that they believe that beer comes out of a printer.' That was his way of saying that, whilst it is possible to put brains on PowerPoint and come up with an answer, it is with brawls on the streets that an answer has to make sense.

The same is true of emotional logic in leadership. It is not enough to talk about compassion and hope, albeit in a compelling way. What we, potential followers, demand is the reassurance that the talk will survive in the real world. What we need to know is that the strategy will be enacted. When we look for leaders we want to know that they not only have a vision but also that they know their business at a level of granularity that is going to enable them to enact that vision.

Shaun O'Callaghan, founder of management research firm Quartet Research, calls this ability to trade a business at a level of granularity 'hand to hand combat'. For a vision to stand any chance of being implemented, executives have to realize that whatever sustainable competitive advantage they think they have will disappear the minute they enter a competitive market.

It is this awareness that competitive advantage never lasts that forces executives to trade their business every day. Without the ability to find this daily differentiation, leaders can become lazy and arrogant. Think of granularity of work as the force that keeps grit of character in check. For followers, this means that to be attractive, leaders must be able to take decisions in the immediacy of the real world rather than in the comfort of the strategic one.

Shaun and I have been looking at this dynamic over the last three years through a small experiment across industries and geographies. We have been sending teams of executives from the same companies to coffee shops in their town, asking them to come back with a number of recommendations for the owner.

There are a number of lessons coming out of the exercise and I'll spare you most of them (if you're a development geek and would like a full run down you'll have to get in touch). There are however three findings I would like to share:

- Finding one: people make two types of recommendations, which they normally call strategic and operational.
- Finding two: the people who make strategic recommendations seldom make operational ones and vice versa.
- Finding three: teams from the same organization tend to make the same kind of recommendations.

So let me explain what I mean by all of this. Assume for a second you are walking into a coffee shop in London. Say it is December. The place is relatively quiet. You notice a couple of members of staff chatting and a few dirty tables. A couple of tables are populated by individuals busy on their laptops with empty coffee cups. Businesspeople and a few tourists are walking past outside. What would you do?

If you are one of the strategy people your recommendations would be about the way the shop looks. The owner professes an authentic Italian experience but there is nothing remotely Italian about the place or the staff. You may recommend a long-term rebranding exercise.

It is also clear that the shop is poorly managed and run. You would probably recommend some review of the organizational structure and some training for the staff and the manager.

You also know that empty coffee cups are not good for business, so you may want to restrict the free wifi or review the service plan to have at least one member of staff walking around asking people if they want any more. You will, of course, have discussed this with your team beforehand. You're not stupid. You do understand that customers are attracted by the low-pressure, comfortable environment. You know all about the so called 'third place' between the office and the home that has made Starbucks so successful. You might even have read Schultz's books for all I know. In fact, scrap that, you are a strategist, you must have read Schultz's books.

You know that increasing the pressure or putting in place inconvenience tactics (eg timed wifi) might alienate the customers you have. But you are a businessperson, you can't help yourself; there are many reasons you find to justify the course of action. Out go the comfy chairs – in go the wifi timers.

You also know that coffee is not your only revenue stream so that the more you sell the better off you are, so in the short term you will introduce a commission/incentive skill for the staff that says that for every muffin or extra they sell they will get a monetary amount (keep it simple, so no percentage just a flat 50 pence). And so come in the endless 'do you want a muffin with that' chants (incidentally if I did want a muffin with that I would have said 'and can I have a muffin with that').

All good recommendations indeed. But what if you are one of the operational people? What would you come up with?

First you probably went to more than the one coffee shop. You probably would have gone to the competition. The question in your mind would be: 'Why should anyone want to buy coffee from me today rather than from someone else?'

Pricing would have been your first port of call. You would have looked at the queuing system to see if everything was in the right place. You would have wanted to clean the tables and to ask the staff to do the same. You would have decided that, given it was a cold day, soup might be a focus so you would recommend dispatching a couple of staff members outside to give out samples. You would have looked at the staff make-up and realized that most were migrant workers, probably more interested in having a great time in London than selling your muffins, so instead of 50 pence for selling a muffin you would put together a competition for free tickets to shows or mobile phone credits.

You might even have recommended writing the name of customers on their loyalty cards so they could be called by their name next time they purchased anything.

Of course all of the above are good recommendations. It is also the case that neither group should be characterized as strategic or operational. Nor is it the case, as is often postulated by development consultants, that one group applied some conceptual long-range thinking whilst others focused on analytical short-range thinking. The problem should be articulated in a different way. One group acted as a group of consultants looking to make recommendations, the other as a group of owners looking to make changes.

Now all good organizations will of course need both of these. However, the issue is that, over time, we have divided them. We have head office people whose job is to be strategic and others with the task of implementation. We have senior people who think and less senior people who do, presumably without having to think.

In our findings Shaun and I also observed that organizations manage talent differently; hence the fact that most people in the same organization tend to approach the coffee shop exercise in a similar way. Whether due to their recruitment, development or performance management processes, over time organizations develop a personality that is either granular or not.

I gained my first degree from the University of St Andrews on the east coast of Scotland. St Andrews is one of the few remaining UK universities where students wear gowns outside graduation. As well as being red, the gown also differs from others in the way it is worn. A first-year student wears it on both shoulders. A second-year student drops one shoulder and a third-year student, two. In the final year the gown comes down to the elbow. I was told in my first year (and who knows if it is true but it seems to fit the arrogance of student life) that this symbolized the fact that the more we filled our brains the less we would have to use our hands. By the fourth year we couldn't move our arms.

This symbolization is present in everyday workplaces. In fact, career transitions and leadership pipelines are characterized by the need to leave habits behind. Sales people need to stop selling when they become sales managers. As we progress through leadership the work becomes influence rather than personal delivery. Micromanagement is inherently seen as bad. Yet it is not as simple as that. Thinking and doing are not separate, and neither are managing and delivering. What counts is the ability of a leader to build credibility through knowing and doing. What counts is the ability to know one's business so well that there is no need for a crib sheet. What counts is not to see the forest for the trees, but to see both the forest and the trees. What counts is to be able to answer the question 'Why should they follow me today?' in a way that makes sense to followers. This takes me back to Anna Maria Tussaud.

To understand the exceptional success of Madame Tussaud, we need to be reminded of the myriad of competing entertainment options of the times. Viewed through a contemporary lens it is easy to assume that she had some kind of sustainable competitive advantage as the only wax artist of her time. This was never the case.

Not only were there a multitude of cabaret and circus acts on offer, all competing for the discretionary time and spend of people, but they were also hundreds of wax artists. And just as in the corporate world today, where skills and knowledge seldom differentiate, so it was in the wax world of her time. They were many Madame Tussauds, yet only one survived. The reason is granularity of work. Madame Tussaud traded her business like no one before her, and she did it by understanding the market to a level of granularity which, each and every day, allowed her to answer the question 'Why should they come to my show rather than anyone else's?'

Step 1: know it

It was not in a studio that Anna Maria Tussaud learnt her trade but the streets of Paris, London and Edinburgh. From the moment that French revolutionaries knocked on the doors of Curtius Studio on their way to the Bastille to borrow effigies of the men they were demonstrating in support of, Anna Maria realized the importance of seeing the world for what it is. Our participants in the coffee shop exercise knew the value of both types of recommendations. The strategic people knew everything the operational ones did. But there are two levels of knowing. One is intellectual and the other visceral. Developing granularity of work means associating curiosity with experience. It means getting your hands dirty in search of knowledge.

The Parisian revolution showed her the need for gore in the same way as the Versailles courts had showed her the need for glory. Anna Maria owed her success to her relentless curiosity. She didn't just develop an instinct for what people wanted, nor did she hold focus groups to ask them. Rather she walked the streets of the places she visited to see for herself what people did. She understood the fascination people had with the fashions of the times, so spent hours on the costumes of the famous as well as on their faces. She saw the need of a nation to know who was important and who wasn't in the political turmoil of the French revolution, changing her exhibits as fast as political favours changed. She was the first to develop a statue of Napoleon when she witnessed at first hand the growing interest in him on the streets of London.

What Anna Maria Tussaud teaches us is the need for a thirst for knowledge stronger than mere curiosity. She wasn't just fascinated or interested; she applied a forensic approach to understanding the times in which she lived – not as a detached professor, but as a field anthropologist. To succeed in igniting emotional logic in their followers, leaders must develop a visceral understanding of issues by walking amongst them. They must see what is going on, not just understand it. Whilst compassion propels us to action, granularity of work targets those actions to the realities of the situation.

Let me give you a concrete example. In most businesses I know, and I am sure this is true in yours, you take pride in your product or service. In fact you take so much pride in your product or service that you use them. You are so faithful that you use them to the exclusion of all others. Of course you know about the competition. You study them. You know their every move. But you see your potential customers rather than studying them, or using them. You may have no idea what it actually feels like to use your competitors' products and services. You know so much that it is possible you analyse at the wrong level of analysis. Granularity of work says that you have to force yourself to know viscerally. You have to feel what your customers feel. As a leader, that's the level of granularity you have to use with potential followers.

Step 2: work it

I talk above about getting your hands dirty in the search for knowledge. Getting her hands dirty is what Anna Maria did as she was forced to rummage through the remains of executed revolutionaries to produce death masks for the rulers of France. She got close to the royals before the revolutionaries by spending time teaching the young princess to make models. She attended the salons of Curtius to observe the philosophers and thinkers of the day in her quest to reproduce them for the masses. Or did she?

As we saw in the opening sentences of this chapter, little is known of Madame Tussaud's life other than what she wanted us to know. We know she probably never was as close to the royal family has she claimed to be. We know that whilst she did indeed do a lot of models of revolutionaries, she is unlikely to have spent time taking their heads out of the guillotine basket. We know that she made models of philosophers, but contrary to her claims we also know that the timings of her claims don't compute. So what are we to make of all of this? Do you have to be a liar to be a leader?

Well no, Madame Tussaud is an extreme example of working the story. She knows that every idea is only as good as the communication that embeds it in the heart of a potential follower. We will come back in the next chapter to the importance of engaging through stories and rhetoric. However, there is one step before that that belongs to asperity and granularity of work. Just as Madame Tussaud had to know it to create it, she had to work it for it to resonate.

Now here is something not many people know. Napoleon wasn't actually short. Indeed he was above average in height. The thing is, French feet and English feet did not measure the same. So whilst Napoleon was 5 ft in France, in English feet that was 5 ft 7 inches, which made him above average for the times. It is easy to see how the constant jokes at his height's expense might account for Napoleon's keen interest in securing a standard unit of measurement (he did leave us the definitive metre measure), but how do we explain the myth of his short stature? Surely others would have spotted the difference?

Maybe they did, but they didn't speak out courtesy of Madame Tussaud. That was another thing she made sure her British audience didn't find out. She needed them to see him as short, as she knew she wasn't selling an effigy but instead was selling an idea that conflict could be won. She was selling the idea of British superiority over the French. She was speaking in the language of implementation. She was making things happen at a level of granularity. It was the accumulation of small ideas drawn from people's lives that strengthened her every day in trading her business through knowing what people were looking for to be engaged. So, no, you don't have to be a liar to be a leader and not all storytelling is fiction. But you have to talk the language of implementation. You have to look for and care about the details – the small things that make a big difference.

Asperity sets the leadership tone. The roughness of character is real whilst the smoothness of manners is learnt. As a result the two often become disconnected. Fatigue, stress and the sheer hard work of leading make demands that an individual's resilience cannot always meet. This is when the disconnect becomes apparent. The mask falls, revealing the ugliness of humanity that the polish of leadership development tried to disguise. It is in these instances that followers sense a lack of integrity. That smooth, mild-mannered, caring and engaging person they call their leader becomes a wreck of contradictions.

You might well have spotted throughout this chapter that asperity relies on one key ally for its success – rhetoric. Being able to express a vision in a way that resonates with the needs of different constituencies is key to igniting emotional logic through charisma. To be resonant, character needs to be expressed. Of course the expression of vision that enthralled many does matter but so does the alignment of that vision with a person's beliefs, thoughts, words and deeds. Both rhetoric and integrity matter. Both are the outward manifestation of the asperity we seek in our leaders. This is why we will look at both in turn in the following two chapters.

> ### The tweet
>
> Leaders aren't smooth operators – roughness of character and a granular understanding of issues makes them attractive to the right followers.

Note

1 The apostrophe was dropped when it became clear everyone used it as part of her name.

CHAPTER 7
RHETORIC

Underpinning question and why it matters

Why does rhetoric matter and how do we use it to ignite emotional logic?

The job of leaders in the character dimension is to influence followers towards a choice. The tool of influence is language. Words form the toolkit of leadership. Words are also what we associate the most with charismatic leaders. We look at them as being great orators. However there is more to rhetoric than public speaking. By knowing how best to construct an argument that resonates at both an intellectual and emotional level, aspiring leaders build the rhetorical skills critical to their success.

In the 19th century your family had to be wealthy for you to go to school. So being born to a draper in the Scottish Border village of Denholm in 1851 ensured that, at 14, James Murray would have to leave full-time education.

However, whilst money might have helped with schooling it wasn't then, and still isn't now, a necessary condition for education. This is where James had an advantage. He was an avid learner – a curious youngster with an enquiring mind and the dedication to fill it with knowledge. Three years after leaving school he was to walk into a new one. This time though he was to teach. Aged 17, James Murray became a teacher at Hawick Grammar School.

Another three years and he was appointed headmaster of Hawick Subscription Academy. Here is our James, six years after leaving school early, and at only 20 becoming a headmaster. That's a fast career but it didn't stop there. Whilst at age 20 James was defying the odds, by age 30 he was defining a language.

James Murray always had a passion for language. Despite taking on a job in a bank he couldn't help pursuing it. When he applied for a job at The British Museum, his letter to Thomas Watts, Keeper of Printed Books, records his fluency in Italian, French, Catalan, Spanish and Latin as well as his working knowledge of Portuguese, Dutch, German, Russian, Hebrew, Slavonic, Syriac, Aramaic and Danish along with Coptic, Phoenician, Anglo-Saxon, Moeso-Gothic, Vaudois, Provençal and various other dialects. And if you are a graduate who happens to be reading this book whilst still searching for a job, just so you know, even with a CV like that, Murray still didn't get the job. So yes, recruiters can be blind to greatness!

Murray eventually got the break he deserved, left the bank and returned to teaching, this time in London, at Mill Hill School. It was there that his continued focus and varied publications on language attracted the attention of the Delegates of the Oxford University Press. On 26 April 1878, they invited him to Oxford to offer him the position of editor of a new dictionary for the English language. The challenge was enormous, the task monumental. The delegates had decided that their dictionary should capture all the English words of all the English world.

It took almost a year for the contract to be signed (so again if you are that graduate reading this, don't despair – HR departments have improved a little but are still notoriously slow). On 1 March 1879, James Murray became the editor of what was to be known as the *Oxford English Dictionary*. The work was planned to take 10 years to publish. They planned four volumes – a total of 7,000 pages.

Murray's first challenge was to work out the mechanics of using almost non-existent resources to catalogue a language spoken all over the world. How do you find out when a word was first used and the context it was used in when there are so many books to consult, so many people to ask? James Murray crowdsourced the task.

Of course no computers means paper and post to transmit the information – a lot of paper and post. In fact, it meant so much paper that after he published appeals for help in newspapers, Murray built a corrugated iron shed in the grounds of Mill Hill School to house the letters he would eventually receive. And he got a lot of them. By the time he moved to Oxford in 1884 the Post Office decided to build a special post box outside his Banbury Road house to facilitate the task of delivering the letters that, by now, were ad- dressed simply to Mr Murray, Oxford. An even bigger shed was duly built in his Oxford garden.

The idea was pure genius. Anyone interested could look up books to spot the use of particular words and write the quotation and its source on a paper slip to be returned to Mr Murray. His assistants would then trawl through the printed slips and cross-reference them in order to find the earliest recorded use of particular words to go alongside the definition. To any of you who see parallels with Wikipedia and its team of editors, you are right: Jimmy Murray, 19th-century Scottish prodigy, was the Jimmy Wales of his times a whole 122 years before Wikipedia!

And just as we find in crowdsourcing and social media today, so the rules of participation were already there in the 19th century. And one particular rule came to prominence: the 1 per cent rule. I wrote about the 1 per cent rule in my last book, *Leadershift*. In short it states that 1 per cent of the people involved in any communal effort have a disproportionately large input to those efforts – Pareto's 80/20 on acid.

Around 1880 a number of contribution slips were starting to arrive. All signed WC Minor, Broadmoor, Crowthorne, Berkshire. For 20 years they never stopped coming. WC Minor became the star contributor to Murray's and his compilers' efforts. But who was this Minor who made no demand and never communi- cated beyond the slips he sent?

As the mountain of slips grew, Murray became intrigued about that most prolific of contributors. Despite the intrigue, it would take 17 years from Minor's first contribution before they met. In 1897 a dinner was arranged. The Great Dictionary Dinner was to bring together all the key contributors to the dictionary. Sadly Minor could not attend. He sent his apologies.

Murray, who still wanted his greatest contributor acknowledged, decided to go and visit the mysterious man to show his appreciation. The large Victorian mansion Murray arrived at on his trip was not the expected grand house of the Victorian gentry; rather it was Broadmoor, the high security psychiatric hospital known then as Broadmoor Criminal Lunatic Asylum, opened some 35 years previously and still operating today at Crowthorne in the Borough of Bracknell Forest in Berkshire, England.

On his arrival, Murray was taken to the Director's office obviously assuming Minor to be the head of the institution. It was not until an inmate was brought in that Murray realized that the man behind the contribution slips was behind bars.

Born on the Island of Ceylon to missionaries from New England, Minor moved to the United States to finish his studies in medicine at the same age as Murray was finishing his studies due to lack of funds. Later accepted by the Union Army as a surgeon, Minor served his country, which he dutifully did until he was allowed to resign his commission in 1870.

Marked by the horrors he saw at the Battle of the Wilderness in 1864, Minor was moved to New York City, where he spent as much time serving his country as he did being served drinks in the seedy bars of the city. The army, becoming worried about his deteriorating mental health, posted him in a remote outpost in Florida before sending him to St Elizabeths Lunatic Asylum in Washington DC.

Having resigned his commission Minor moved to the UK in 1871, where he settled into what was then known as the slum of Lambeth in London (British readers might be tempted to draw a comic parallel between Lambeth then and now but I won't). It was there that he was found not guilty by reason of insanity of the murder of George Merrett, a father of six children married to a pregnant Eliza Merrett. Merrett had been on his way to work when a deluded Minor was convinced Merrett was going to mug him and shot him to death.

Minor was incarcerated in Broadmoor where he was allowed to buy and read books. It was through his numerous interactions with London's booksellers that he heard of Murray's call for help. He had a lot of time on his hands and a full library at his disposal (made even larger by Eliza, Merrett's wife who took pity on him at the trial and visited him, bringing books as gifts). He devoted his time to the task of contributing to the dictionary from the time he heard the call until the end of his life.[1]

Sadly neither Murray nor Minor would live to see the publication of the finished *Oxford English Dictionary*. By the time the dictionary was finally published, the 10 years' planned completion timescale had turned to almost 50 and the four volumes had become 12. A monument to language, the *Oxford English Dictionary* defined 414,825 words with 1,827,306 citations used throughout to illustrate their meaning. Murray the Scot and Minor the American had finally defined the English language. What they didn't know is that, in so doing, they had just published the first leadership book.

Words are the tools of leadership. My good friend Tom Hood, the Executive Director and CEO of the Maryland Association of CPAs, likes to say the leaders are readers.[2] He is right but let me take it one step further and say that great leaders are not only great readers, they are great speakers and writers. In fact, they are not speakers as in great platform evangelists or writers as in award-winning journalists or novelists, but rather great speakers and writers as those who influence with words. We like to say that actions speak louder than words or that facts and data speak for themselves, but actually you cannot separate actions from words, nor facts from stories.

The way we think about events in our lives (cognitions) determines how we feel about them (emotions) and the way we feel about them determines the way we respond (actions). The way an argument is formed is not just a matter of style; it is a matter of how it is understood and felt and therefore acted upon. Rhetoric, the way an argument is made, is key to influencing choice and therefore navigating the character dimension of emotional logic.

Before I go any further, let me explain why I have just taken up your valuable time with the story of Murray and Minor, other than of course out of the sheer historical interest of a tale worthy of any quiz you may attend in the future. The reason I wanted Murray and Minor to open this chapter for us is because in many ways they defined everything yet somehow they defined nothing. Remember our duck that was ready to eat in Chapter 2. You can understand all the words and the grammar can be correct, yet the sentence still doesn't make any sense without context. It is why I like to think of the dictionary as the leader's toolkit. Tools alone don't make anything; the competence of the craftsman is what accounts for the outcome. In the case of words it is rhetoric that provides a meaning to whatever these words are used to create.

In fact we act on the basis of what we hear, not what is said. I like to give the example of my son putting too much salt on his food at the dinner table. I could explain the disadvantages of high quantities of salt and ask him to stop. In the heat of the moment, I am afraid to say, all I say is 'oh George'. That simple sentence (even when uttered with no urgency, a friendly tone and a smile) always seems to work. George knows (through his personal experiences and our shared history) that 'oh George' stands for 'Stop whatever it is you are doing now as it's probably not a good thing.' George, in this situation, acts, not on the actual meaning of the words, but on the meaning he attaches to the words – what linguists call an indirect speech act.

Both networks of association and indirect speech acts tell us that there is more to the story of influencing than words. They tell us that the way words are used and the context they are used in is as important, if not more so, to leadership. Murray understood the importance of context; this is why he enlisted an army of 'Minors' to provide the necessary context. By asking them to pinpoint the date and context of first use through quotations, Murray defined the words but Minor made them come to life. Making words come to life is what leaders need to do to ignite emotional logic. For people to make the choice to follow, they must be moved to do so by the leader. Persuading and influencing people through speech (rather than making speeches) is what rhetoric is about (its etymology is in the Greek for orator).

The Greek philosopher Aristotle defined rhetoric as 'the ability, in each particular case, to see the available means of persuasion.' It was not until later in the 16th century that the depreciatory meaning of the word first appeared. Unfortunately for us it is that negative connotation that is prominent in the business world. Just as design is often thought of as making something pretty (regardless of whether or not it has inherent beauty) or marketing as making something desirable (regardless of whether it is or not), for many, rhetoric is just the art of lying cleverly or speaking artificially to make something appealing. This is not what I am talking about here. Rhetoric is not about lies. Aristotle provides us with three important areas of focus necessary for any argument to influence:

- Logos – influencing using logic, reasons and facts to support a claim.
- Pathos – influencing through emotion and motivation.
- Ethos – influencing through character and credibility.

It's no surprise that these three elements align perfectly to the description and the workings of emotional logic we looked at in part one. Leaders are resonant because they appeal to our rational (logos) and emotional (pathos) sides through their character (ethos). It is the argument they make that helps us make choices. These three strands of Aristotelian rhetoric come together to form arguments – leaders make coherent (logos), compelling (pathos) and credible (ethos) arguments (Figure 7.1). All three steps matter in influencing others towards a goal.

Figure 7.1 The three facets of an argument that unlock rhetoric

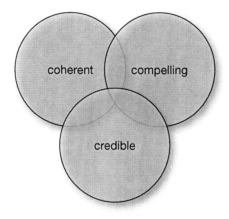

Stage 1: coherent – building a valid and sound argument

As I mentioned above rhetoric is not about lying (albeit cleverly and beautifully). To sustain influence, leaders must have a coherent argument to make. It has to stand up to scrutiny. You will find countless examples of arguments made that seem appealing but are flawed (the world of politics is a good place to go to if you're looking). As we saw in Part II when we looked at the values dimension underpinned by compassion and hope, potential followers, in the long term, will need reassurance that the vision is achievable. They require an argument that is both understandable and believable.

Making the argument understandable

Building an argument is the same as building a story – a narrative. Many of us share a flawed belief that facts speak for themselves. But they don't. There are too many facts that speak and the resulting noise means they are impossible to hear clearly. The narrative is the argument. It is about putting the facts in a context that helps understanding.

We understand our world through narratives. When we receive information we organize it into a story – a structure – that helps us make sense of it. A spreadsheet or a series of bullet points leaves the receiver to create a narrative. Inspiring leaders do not leave the narrative to chance – they create it.

All narratives obey a structure – a plot. That plot is the argument. The narrative structure contains a set-up, a conflict and a resolution. To lead is to narrate. It is about organizing facts in a way that sets up the challenge, builds the tension and leads to a resolution.

To make an argument coherent we must work not only at the logical level but also at the narrative level. In my practice I advise people to think in terms of a storyboard for any argument they make. I ask them to think about the narrative first. What is the story they are trying to tell? Why does it matter? What are the choices that need to be made and why? How can we resolve the conflict we face?

Once you have the narrative structure you use your premises to build the plot. The best way to do this is to stand away from the data and talk about what it means. This does not mean that you have to massage the facts to fit the story or find new facts that fit. Rather it means you have to be clear about what you want the audience to take away from the facts.

Facts do indeed matter. In fact, the problem with the word 'stories' is that many of us equate it with the word 'fiction'. So whilst an argument must have a narrative structure it does not mean it has to be untrue. The second element of building a coherent argument is believability, and this is where logic comes in.

Making the argument believable

There are broadly two types of logic that are used to make arguments. One is deductive, the other inductive. An argument made using deductive logic is one where the conclusion necessarily follows from a set of premises. The famous 'all men are mortal, Socrates is a man, therefore Socrates is mortal' is a prime example of deductive logic. If our premises are right/true then the conclusion cannot in any way be wrong/false. An inductive argument, on the other hand, is one where the premises are used as good reasons for holding a conclusion as being true. In an inductive argument, even correct premises can lead to a wrong conclusion (the premise/conclusion link is weaker). For example all living things we know of depend on water to live, therefore all living things depend on water to live. We go from a generality to a conclusion without potentially accounting for exceptions (ie the living things we might not know about that may not require water to live).

What both of these types of reasoning have in common, and the very reason I mention them here, is that they highlight the two areas that are critical to making an argument – the premises and the inference/conclusion. Some arguments may be valid (ie the reasoning is correct) without being sound (ie the premises are wrong). To influence through coherence (reasons and facts) we need to ensure that our arguments (the logic and premises) stand up to scrutiny, not just our conclusions. Like maths teachers asking to see your workings not just your conclusion, influencing others means taking them on a journey not just showing them a destination. And if the destination is appealing then the journey must take us there.

To build coherence you need to challenge your argument at two levels. Is it true and is it believable? That second level is too often forgotten as leaders have access to a lot of information that followers will never see. As a result they make deductive and inductive logical leaps followers can never make.

Too often this translates into what I call a PowerPoint vision – a set of slides that tell us the world is going to end and the only way forward is to follow the leader's path. The trouble is that the PowerPoint (even if covered with bullet points as they often are) cannot capture all the premises and the logical steps taken by the leader. As a result we skip a few steps, show a couple of stop signs and locations, and then put up the pretty picture of the beach-fronted house we always aimed to reach. How you got from A to B is still a mystery to the audience you are looking to influence.

Making a cogent argument that is both valid and sound is about understanding the flow of the logic. An argument is more than a set of disjointed scenes. The key to making an argument believable is to ensure premises are clear for followers and follow the link between the premises and inferences to build the narrative.

The very essence of emotional logic is that conscious rationality alone does not drive decision making. We have seen in previous chapters how reason and emotions cannot be separated. We believe that the right facts should influence the right action. Yet, at the same time, even with a clear narrative we know that some people will not act rationally. Doctors spend their careers giving people facts and narratives about what will happen without a change of behaviour only to witness people carrying on doing what is harmful to them. The reality, as we have seen, is that logic alone does not move us. Movement comes from emotions, which is why stage 2, making an argument compelling, matters.

Stage 2: compelling – building an argument that resonates

In rhetoric, pathos deals with an appeal to emotions. It moves an argument from being coherent to being compelling.

In 1986, the British newspaper the *Guardian* ran an advert that not only won prizes but disturbed the notions of a nation. Created by the Boase Massimi Pollitt agency, the advert was called 'point of view' and formed part of a broader campaign entitled 'wider perspectives'. In it you saw a skinhead run at speed past a woman. In the second shot, the skinhead rushed towards a business man. He jumped on him as the business man tried to protect himself by holding up his briefcase. It is only when the shot expands that you realize that your assumption that the skinhead was about to steal the briefcase was in fact wrong. As the camera panned out, it became clear that the skinhead had spotted a load of building material about to fall on the business man and was rushing to push him out of the way of an assured death.

The ad ran for 30 seconds and the narrative was compelling. Accompanying the stark black and white pictures the voiceover simply said: 'an event seen from one point of view gives one impression, seen from another point of view it gives quite a different impression, but it's only when you get the whole picture you can fully understand what's going on.' The ad closed with the guardian logo and a simple tag line – 'the whole picture'.

That advert goes to the core of how we view the world. It shows how interpretation is dependent both on our state of mind and our point of view. As observers we are reliant on our points of view. And as we saw earlier, the job of rhetoric is to help a leader create the narrative so as to drive our interpretation. There are two questions to ask to build resonant narratives.

What frame will you adopt?

People who are fond of saying that the facts speak for themselves haven't heard of frames. Frames are the constructs we rely on to understand and respond to events and arguments (through their advert the *Guardian* was exploding our frames). They are the filters through which we understand the world. Framing communications means building a narrative in a way that encourages the choice of certain interpretations over others.

Cognitive and mathematical psychologist Amos Tversky and psychologist and Nobel laureate Daniel Kahneman best demonstrated the effect of framing in a classic experiment. Participants were asked to 'imagine that the US is preparing for the outbreak of an unusual Asian disease, which is expected to kill 600 people. Two alternative programs to combat the disease have been proposed. Assume the exact scientific estimate of the consequences of the programs are as follows.'

One group of participants in the experiment were given the choice of two programmes to adopt:

- With programme A: '200 people will be saved.'
- With programme B: 'there is a one-third probability that 600 people will be saved, and a two-thirds probability that no people will be saved.'

Given that choice, 72 per cent of participants went for the certainty of saving lives offered by programme A.

The second group of participants was presented with a different choice.

- They were told that with programme C: '400 people will die.'
- With Programme D: 'there is a one-third probability that nobody will die, and a two-third probability that 600 people will die.'

This group rejected the certainty of death offered by programme C, with 78 per cent opting for programme D.

Of course, having seen all four programmes, you and I know that programmes A and C are identical, as are programmes B and D. The only thing that is different is the frame offered. For the first group, programme A felt more secure than C as it referred to lives saved.

This is common in the way we make choices. All choices are a balance between risk tolerance and reward anticipation. And as the example above illustrates we prefer certainty over risk when facing a likely gain (as with programme A). However when a choice is framed with likely loss (as in programme B), we tend to exhibit more risk-averse behaviours. Altering the frame from positive (certainty of lives saved) to negative (certainty of lives lost), rewards leaders with more risk-taking behaviours.

The importance for leaders is to understand that arguments can and should be framed to elicit a choice. As we build our narratives so too should we build our frames. By framing the problem, the solution and the call to action of our narrative, we ensure the interpretation of our argument is not left to chance. We also increase the odds of the relevant behaviour arising from our rhetoric. Understanding that people have frames, and that the way you frame an argument is key to influencing their choices, is key to rhetorical success.

How do you ignite that frame?

You may recall that, when talking about my children and the duck, I mentioned that I could have primed their response by igniting some networks of association (either to do with the duck as food, or the duck as pet). There are countless examples of the effect of priming, from students who unconsciously walk more slowly and hold themselves less straight after being showed images of older people[3] to others who find it harder to pass a test after being exposed to stereotypical images and texts relating to football hooligans, and easier when primed with references related to professors.[4]

Priming ensures we ignite certain networks of association (the *Guardian*'s skinhead primed our 'danger neurons'). Words as well as images can prime. Changing the name 'inheritance tax' to 'death tax', or using 'climate change' rather than 'global warming' primes different responses. The choice of language is key when making an argument. One of the most effective rhetorical devices for framing and priming is metaphors.

Too often we think of metaphors as nice flourishes to use in communications. They are the proverbial lipstick on the pig. That is far from true. Metaphors shape our understanding. We use them to orientate our behaviour. What makes metaphors powerful in rhetoric is that they require the listener to do the work. You cannot accept a metaphor passively. Your brain gets to work in understanding what is in the container.

We know that framing is stronger if it fits within an individual's belief system. By using metaphors we give the receiver of our argument the opportunity to test a frame against that belief system. The choice of metaphors we use therefore reinforces a frame. That's why the best leaders use metaphors. They know that metaphors activate your networks of association and lead you to action.

But while coherent and compelling arguments help people make a follower-ship choice they also, by their very nature, expand and distort reality. Their effectiveness or otherwise will therefore be dependent on the credibility of the speaker. Whilst a message may be believable, it is its source that makes it credible. This is why the third stage to unlocking rhetoric matters.

Stage 3: credible – building reassurance in our argument

As we saw in my son and salt example earlier, any argument rests or falls on the basis of who is making it. The credibility of the source makes the argument credible. David Berlo, communication expert and consultant, identified three elements of credibility – expertise, trustworthiness and dynamism. I like to describe these with the formula shown in Figure 7.2. Let's take each to uncover how they work.

Figure 7.2 The credibility formula

Trustworthiness

The consultant to other consultants David Maister highlights a number of factors that determine trust. In particular he talks about intimacy, reliability and the importance of what he calls a lack of self-orientation. In short we are more likely to trust people with whom we feel we have a connection (intimacy), who do what they say (reliability) and are more motivated by what's in it for us rather than what it's in for them (lack of self-orientation).

By highlighting elements of your personal history and understanding that of others through compassion, you will build intimacy. Being open about the premises of your argument also increases reliability. But above all for our purpose here, the important factor is the lack of self-orientation. While a leader might do most of the talking the discussion needs to be follower-focused. The argument doesn't try to sell anything other than reassurance. Followers must feel that it is for their benefit, not the leader's.

We know when someone is trying to sell us something for their own benefit. We know when leaders act in their own interest not ours. We have an inbuilt self-orientation detector. You cannot fake interest in others. You cannot hide self-orientation. To avoid creating those feelings in others, aspiring leaders need to think about a line I have used repeatedly throughout my consulting career. That line is a question: 'Have I made him/her/them feel stronger and more capable?'

Expertise

The other part of credibility is expertise. Does the person know what they are talking about? There are two ways to judge this. One is objective. You can test for expertise. The second is subjective. It has more to do with those white lab coats – the trappings of expertise. The biggest trapping of expertise is language. We expect leaders to understand the language we use and to use a language we understand, but we also expect them to use the language of expertise.

Whilst we can all list our 'qualifications', the key is to speak in a way followers understand, teaching them the language of our expertise. I find that expertise is a particular challenge to aspiring leaders who are early in their career. Few understand the expertise of leadership – and find it hard relying on professional expertise when others around them are potentially better experts. The key to expertise is understanding what yours is. What is your actual value added and what are the proof points to that value added? A key task for leaders is to be able to articulate what defines them as leaders.

Dynamism

The final element of credibility is dynamism. Berlo himself wasn't sure he should have included it in his model of credibility (on the basis that although it influences credibility it does so potentially only through likeability). I have decided to include it here as I believe it makes an important contribution to rhetoric, but as you can see from the equation, it is not a multiplier but rather an addition to credibility. Dynamism is both a thirst for sharing knowledge and an ability to tailor that knowledge to the right audience.

One is about being able to convey the passion for your subject, topic or vision and the other is about doing so in a language people understand. Passion can be made visible by talking with conviction. Leaders must be excited about their vision (by which I do not mean jumping around but rather exuding a sense that they too want to get there). But dynamism also means reacting to followers and their questions.

Leaders are not only passionate about their vision and dynamic in the way they present it (with a sense of urgency and conviction), but they are also multi-lingual translators, able to flex the language of their expertise to the language of their audience.

We have seen so far how successfully navigating the character dimension depends on a leader's ability to sell a compelling vision through asperity and rhetoric. It is easy to see how both of these interact (you cannot sell a vision unless you stand for something). The character dimension enables followers to develop a belief that following is safer than not. It helps them gauge whether the benefits of followership outweigh the risk of surrendering their goals to another person. There is therefore another piece missing that helps followers character define. We have started to touch upon it in our last two elements (asperity and rhetoric) and that is integrity, which is where we are going next.

The tweet

Leaders are orators. Masters of rhetoric, their arguments are coherent (logic), compelling (emotions) and credible (character).

Notes

1   You can read a fuller account of Minor's life and contribution in Simon Winchester's *The Professor and the Madman: A tale of murder, insanity, and the making of the Oxford English Dictionary* (Harper Perennial, 2005).

2   He does like to say a lot of important things, my friend Tom. In fact he also says that success for leaders can be written as L>C, meaning that a leader's rate of learning has to be superior to the environment's rate of change. I like that a lot, and for more of Tom's wisdom until he writes his own book, you can follow him on twitter @tomhood.

3   Bargh, JA, Chen, M and Burrows L (1996) 'Automaticity of social behavior: direct effects of trait construct and stereotype activation on action', *Journal of Personality and Social Psychology*, **71** (2), pp 230–44.

4   Dijksterhuis, A and van Knippenberg, A (1998) 'The relation between perception and behavior, or how to win a game of trivial pursuit', *Journal of Personality and Social Psychology*, **74** (4), pp 865–77.

CHAPTER 8
INTEGRITY

Underpinning question and why it matters

Why is integrity key to charisma and how is it tested by followers?

By now, followers have tested the potential leader for the necessary grit to remain true to a vision (asperity) and the ability to demonstrate this force of character (rhetoric). There is another test that followers apply to a leader's character. This test is integrity. Integrity is the element that helps followers measure a leader's ability to keep his/her word. I defined the character dimension as being the answer to the question: 'Will the potential leader have what it takes to act in line with my values?' Integrity is the ultimate test of whether deeds are in line with words. Without that alignment no trust is possible.

It's amazing how song lyrics can make their way, seemingly out of nowhere, to the forefront of our minds. On one cold morning in London it was John Lennon's words that resonated in my head. A little girl was being comforted by her mother. She was crying with a mixture of sadness and fear in her eyes. The scene was distressing. John Lennon was providing the lyrics and Bryan Ferry the voice. 'I didn't mean to hurt you. I'm sorry that I made you cry'[1] was going around in my head. I didn't know her. We had never spoken or even seen each other before. Yet her distress was all my fault.

If you think that's a pretty weird scene to start a chapter with, wait until I tell you how we got there. At the time, I was standing in the Westfield shopping mall in Shepherds Bush, London, just outside the 'Build-a-Bear workshop' store. The little girl was crying because she was afraid to go into this store. Any of you who have ever seen or visited a Build-a-Bear store will know that there are many emotions and noises displayed by children there. There may even be tears as parents try to restrain their children from spending an entire month's wages on the goods on display. But fear is not an emotion often associated with the Build-A-Bear emporium.

The little girl, however, was clearly afraid to go in. Her fear was reasonable. 'But mummy', she kept repeating, 'it's full of old men'. And it was. The Build-a-Bear store had been invaded that morning by 25 executives from a multi-national who were participating in one of the workshop's notorious birthday parties. It wasn't anyone's birthday. It was a learning experience and I was partly responsible for having organized it. It's fair to say that the little girl had missed the couple of female executives who were there and had over-estimated the average age. Yet, there was no denying that there was something frightening about a group of executives holding teddy bears above their heads whilst chanting in unison 'Dress my bear'.

All I can say in my defence is that there was a good reason why I, along with my clients and helped by a retail experience consultant, had chosen to take the 25 executives there that morning. And much of that had to do with the next stage of our walk through charisma – integrity.

For those of you not familiar with the Build-a-Bear experience, the company was started by Maxine Clark, or to give her her official title 'Founder, Chairman and Chief Executive Bear', in 1997 in St Louis, Missouri. As is the case with many late 20th-century companies this one too has a cute story to accompany its creation. Maxine was taking a child shopping for a bear. The child, disappointed by the lack of choice and the fact that she could not find the exact bear she wanted, suggested they should make one up. Rather than crafting a bear however, Maxine decided to craft a business plan. When the child talked about creating a bear, Maxine's interpretation was to create a workshop to make them. She wasn't about to reinvent the teddy bear. As she puts it: 'After all, Ray Kroc from McDonald's didn't invent hamburgers and Howard Schultz from Starbucks didn't invent coffee, they just invented how to sell more and how to sell it better.' This would be her mission: sell more and sell better. The Build-a-Bear workshop was born.

When entering a Build-a-Bear workshop, you enter a process. The process has a number of clearly identified steps, each occupying a different part of the store and each clearly indicated by a large sign in blue letters on a yellow background. At the 'choose me' stage a child will choose an animal from an endless and constantly changing collection of available skins. At the 'hear me' stage they will decide if they want the bear to make a noise and the nature of that noise from a selection of available sounds. They can even record their own sound if they want.

The bear is then brought to life at the 'stuff me' stage where bear builders will use a big machine to stuff the bear in front of the child. But then something even more magical happens to bring the bear to life. The child is given a small heart made out of red fabric and goes through a number of steps to bring the heart and the bear to life. First the heart must be warmed between the hands (who doesn't want a warm-hearted bear), then the heart is stroked on the cheeks (we want our bear to be a little bit cheeky), the heart is wiped over the forehead (we want our bear to have brains) and arms (we want our bears to be strong)… you get the idea. Eventually, the child closes her eyes and makes a wish prior to the heart being put inside the bear. From then on, it's no longer *a* bear. It is now *her* bear!

Duly stuffed teddy is now brushed ('fluff me') and named ('name me'). Having printed the birth certificate, children move on to the 'dress me' stage. There, they can choose from a variety of accessories ranging from shirts to mobile phones via hats and shoes. Finally at the 'take me home' stage, the bear is put in a box shaped like a house whilst the parents pay. The whole thing then climaxes in the child making 'the bear promise' of always looking after her 'beary' best friend for life.

You may cringe at the over-the-top nature of it all when reading those lines. I have lived in the UK long enough to know that, at least, most Brits would. However, as experience retail goes, on a global scale, Build-a-Bear is unmatched. It might also be worth noting that even fully grow-up Brits get caught up in the experiential nature of it all. Maxine Clark has been the recipient of a multitude of awards, from being named one of the 25 most influential people in retailing by *Chain Store Age* magazine to being elected Customer-Centred Leader by *Fast Company* magazine. Her business was named Best Company to Work For by *Fortune* magazine and Portfolio Company of the Year by the National Association of Small Business Investment Companies. Build-a-Bear workshop has now grown from its one store in Saint Louis Galleria to over 400 stores worldwide with over 70 million bears sold around the globe.

It was that retailing success that had brought the 25 executives and me to the Westfield shopping mall. We were trying to understand the nature of unmatched customer experiences and, in its field, Build-a-Bear is pretty unmatched. The idea was for the team of executives to be taken through a birthday party experience similar to those hosted at Build-a-Bear. We would go through the process, build our bears and afterwards try to understand what made it such a draw for children of all ages. We would also look at the model to work out why, in a mall where shops are located by category, Build-a-Bear could afford to sell a bear for roughly four times the amount the Disney store next door was charging for nearly identical ones. In a commoditized world where only experiences differentiate, how did Build-a-Bear do it? It is our findings that taught me something about the character dimension of emotional logic and integrity in particular that I want to share with you.

Having looked at the prospective leader's ability to stay true to followers' espoused values through strength and grit of character (asperity) as well as their ability to articulate what they stand for (rhetoric), emotional logic's attention now turns to a critical test of character. At this stage in their follower-ship decision-making process, followers need to understand that what the potential leader says is indeed aligned to what they think and will do. Followers need to understand that the leader has integrity. Integrity is key to charisma and provides the trust we need to let ourselves be led. It is also often misunderstood in leadership. And as strange as it may seem, the Build-a-Bear workshop is a lesson in integrity.

Think of any retail experiences you have had. What separates a merely average experience from a great one? Is it about the staff not being engaged, the purchase process being too complicated, the shop being messy? Whatever else it might be, it always comes back to one fundamental element – a gap between the promise and the reality. The experiences we value the most are the experiences that deliver and hopefully exceed our expectations. We value experiences that are true to their word. Experiences that are true to their word have integrity.

What makes Build-a-Bear such an attractive case study in retail experience is that the entire concept has integrity. The experience is designed from the ground up. The sales process is indistinguishable from the experience. Most organizations view experiences in the same way they view design. They see it as a bit of glitter you put on top of the cake to make it pretty. At Build-a-Bear, the cake itself is the experience. The recruitment process, a kind of *American Idol*-type audition, is an integral part of the experience. The Customer Relationship Management system is part of the 'name me' process. The experience feels genuine because it is genuine. It is genuine because it is integrated.

It is that integration and alignment that makes Build-a-Bear the right starting point for a chapter on integrity. Integrity is often used in leadership conversations. Most models of leadership contain a requirement for integrity. Yet, both conversations and models are found wanting as integrity is a confusing attribute. Looking for definitions of integrity will invariably lead to moral and ethical considerations, the very conflicting and contradictory nature of which end up setting a movable bar impossible for most to reach. Build-a-Bear offers an example of the most prescient definition of integrity applicable to emotional logic. In the Build-a-Bear context, integrity is devoid of moral content. Integrity is not about good or bad but rather is defined as unity. Integrity is about the alignment and predictability of the experience. Integrity is about followers having the trust that what is said will be done – the experience is true to the promise.

Of course, I am not saying that morals and ethics do not matter in leadership, business or life. However, they are not part of the test of the character dimension of emotional logic. It is under the values dimension that followers will look at what constitutes an attractive vision of the future. While, as I mentioned before, there is no guarantee that what followers decide will match what others may deem to be moral and ethical, it is at that stage that moral and ethical considerations will take place. The character dimension of emotional logic is trying to ascertain the likelihood that the leaders will stick to their word on the journey towards achieving their vision of hope. History, as I postulated, is full of leaders who have been successfully followed even when their moral stance was questionable, but what has integrity in the context of charisma is what has completeness, not necessarily morality.

By integrity I mean the alignment we witness at Build-a-Bear. The integrity test is a test of that alignment. At Build-a-Bear we witness three important elements of alignment. The business model is aligned to a sales process, which in turn is aligned to an experience. Similarly when we look at leadership there are a number of elements that need to be linked.

The values dimension of emotional logic helps followers gauge whether you understand them and the hope you propose to provide. The character dimension helps them understand whether you have what it takes to deliver. Asperity provides the litmus test of your ability to stand for something, and rhetoric helps you articulate what it is you stand for. The role of integrity is to link all this together. It provides the alignment between what you think you can do (your intent) and what you say you want to do (your word), and it gives an indication as to what you will do (your actions, which we will turn to in the achievement dimension). There are two stages in building this alignment. The first is to understand the importance of your word and how to demonstrate it. I call this the 'stating and demonstrating your word' stage. The second stage is about the alignment of your actions against the experience you wish to deliver for your followers. For reasons that will become clear later I call this second element 'restating your word'.

Stage 1: stating and demonstrating your word

I defined integrity as being aligned against a promise. Essentially, followers will need to determine whether you will act in line with what you say. There is however a first step prior to acting in line with what you say. That step is to mean what you say.

This step is a strange one to highlight. In many ways it seems obvious that if you mean what you say you are much more likely to act in accordance with it. Yet it also seems an unnecessary step. If followers rely on you acting on what you say to test your integrity, the only test should be that you say it with sufficient conviction and act in line with that conviction. After all there is no need for you to really mean it. It would appear that all we need is to go straight from our previous chapter on rhetoric to the last chapter on action. However this would be ignoring the fact that lack of authenticity is not only easily detected by followers but also derails us in our actions.

Let's go back to Build-a-Bear. To be successful, the experience relies on both how you receive it and how it is delivered to you. On the face of it we could argue that who provides the experience is pretty much irrelevant as long as you experience it as positive. Indeed the fact that the experience is actually designed in the sales process means that we only need to script the interaction for it to feel good. Yet, having been through the experience with a number of groups I can assure you this is not the case. Human beings, as we previously saw, are very well versed in sensing inauthenticity. It is the small things that lead to the erosion of this authenticity. A member of staff who oversells or one with a forced smile are all small indications of something inauthentic – and inauthenticity destroys the sense of integrity.

Of course, there are processes you can put in place to ensure that authenticity stays in place. For example Build-a-Bear do not commission their staff. They are only rewarded on the basis of the experience, as gauged through customer feedback and mystery shopping, not on sales figures. This ensures they have you rather than your wallet in their mind at all times. But no process can actually ensure that people are authentic in the delivery of an experience. This can only be done if they have an emotional rather than a contractual connection to their work.

The manager of the shop I visited in London had a simple way to reconnect employees with their emotions. He called it the 'wall of why'. At the back of the store, in the corridor leading to the front, an odd assortment of pictures and keepsakes is posted on the wall. At first glance it appears as though someone couldn't afford the kind of interior designer that makes the Google and Facebook offices of this world look groovy, so decided to have a go themselves. But on closer inspection you may recognize some of the staff in the pictures. Chris, the store manager, explains the 'wall of whys' simply as 'the reasons we come to work everyday'.

Some people might come to work in order to buy a car or afford a dream holiday so they will put on the wall pictures, cut out of magazines, of their dream car or destinations. Others may come to work to provide a better education for their children, in which case they will put photos of the kids on the wall. Whatever has made them make the journey to work everyday is on the wall. And the wall is on the way to the front of the store. This means that every time someone comes out to see you in the store they have just walked past the biggest emotional reminder of why they are here.

I think the 'wall of why' is a pretty neat idea to encourage people to reconnect with their emotions in order to spread them. I also can't help but wonder how many of these emotional connections many businesses have lost in implementing clean-desk policies to facilitate 'hot desking'. But there is something else of importance that is represented by the 'wall of whys'. It helps us create a framework for integrity. Integrity is, in effect, a framework built on clarity. It starts with clarity of intent. Your promise needs to be clear in your head if it is to be clearly stated to others. Stating it means not only being clear in what you say but being clear in what others understand. Finally you need to be clear on what it means for your word to be enacted. Together these steps ensure integrity. It is the breakdown between them that leads to lack of trust on the part of potential followers. So let's take each of those steps in turn.

Step 1: being clear on your promise

This first step is our 'wall of whys'. By now you will have done a lot of thinking about the reason for your leadership, identified in the values dimension, and also your ability to deliver on your promise, as gauged by asperity and rhetoric. The key to this first step is that you now need to translate this into your promise. Being able to articulate an agenda clearly will help followers be clear on your promise.

In our last chapter on rhetoric we looked at the broad outlines of what you stand for, but here we need to translate this into an agenda. Are you able to summarize the four key priorities you want to focus on? It could be three or six but it really shouldn't be 10, otherwise it's hard to see these as priorities. Are you sure these are the right things to focus on? Are they make-or-break deals for you? Because if they are not, you are unlikely to stick to them and therefore will be viewed as lacking integrity. Once we have the list we need to turn to how we articulate it.

Step 2: articulating and demonstrating your word

Having decided on your priorities you need to be able to articulate them in a way that will create clarity for your followers – not just clarity of intent but clarity of actions. For each of your priorities you should be able to articulate some things that can be done to demonstrate them. In effect Step 1 is about the articulation of the Build-a-Bear process and the stages within this – choose me, stuff me and so on – while Step 2 is the explanation of what will happen at each stage.

In order to enable your followers to decide whether you have integrity you need to give them a way to judge past actions as well as to measure future ones. By articulating each of your priorities and giving an indication of some of the actions that underpin them, you should also be able to demonstrate instances when things have worked out. At this stage it is important that you look back at the values dimension to ensure that what you propose is in line with what you have established your followers aspire to.

So this is your word and you had better stick to it. But will you? Anyone who knows anything about being human knows that only people who do very little stand the chance of always delivering against their promises. So what happens on the occasions when you fail?

Stage 2: restating your word

There is a second stage in our integrity story, which I call 'restating your word'. There are two reasons why I chose this particular title. The first is that, never mind how many times you say something, the pressures of everyday lives, mixed with the sheer amount of communication people are exposed to, mean your potential followers will forget what you say. In this context, restating your word, simply and often, will maximize the chances of integrity.

The second reason is somewhat less obvious but in many ways more important. If we define integrity as delivering on the promise of your word, what happens when you don't deliver? The world is too complex, situations too varied and leadership context too changeable to believe that you will always fulfil your promises. It is also fair to say that human beings are not consistent machines. We have quirks of behaviour. We have off days. We have distractions. To talk about integrity without talking about these potential failures is to ignore human nature.

To carry on with our retail experience analogy, let's think for a moment about what happens when a business fails to deliver against its promises. We have all been there. We have all experienced the parcel that never arrives, the cheque that is in the post or the product that fails. As David Williams, retail experience expert and CEO of the aptly name consultancy 'How to Experience', taught me, when looking at a failure to deliver, businesses will always ask two questions. Question one is 'whose fault was it?' Question two is 'how serious is the problem?' Of course if you are a business person reading this you will know that all service strategies are designed along these two continua, providing one of those neat two by twos we consultants love so much.

If the problem is your fault and not that important, you apologize and fix it. If the problem is more important, you will have some form of service recovery procedure with some kind of red-carpet treatment attached. The whole thing becomes most interesting when you actually didn't create the problem. That's where true customer service can be tested and integrity brought back. If the problem is not that serious, I am pretty sure you will have trained your service personnel in the art of demonstrating empathy. If the problem is serious and you didn't create it, things do, however, become that little bit more intriguing. What are you to do? At Build-a-Bear they integrate a tag into the bear so that if it is found by someone it can be returned to its rightful owner. A child losing a bear is not Build-a-Bear's fault, and as every parent can attest it is indeed a big deal. Solving the big problems that are not your fault is the stuff of legendary service. Yet, in a rush to solve cases that are your fault, the likelihood is that those that are not will be ignored.

Most businesses will never deviate from this approach to customer recovery. The reason is that they find it hard not to defend their business at the same time as trying to get customers back on their side. That's why the letters of apology invariably start with the dreaded 'I am sorry on that occasion our service levels fell short of our usual high standards' or some such phrase that tells you that you are the exception rather than the rule. Whilst this terminology is designed to reassure, it also points to a kind of complacency. It highlights that the problem is not as important as the customer may feel. It suggests that the customer's problem is small by the very fact that it is one in a million. It fails to understand that for that 'one in a million' the problem is the only one that counts. More importantly it forgets that it is memories that engender loyalty, and knowing that you have the wrong memory does not in and of itself help solve the issue.

The reason I took a detour through what business academics and consultants call 'customer-recovery strategies' and normal human beings call 'caring' is that they are integrity-testing moments. They are the moments customers use to gauge the character of a business through its integrity. Will the business lead by its promise and realign the experience to my expectations? What is true of customers is true of followers, and what is true of businesses is true of leaders.

Anyone who is called upon to lead, will, at some stage, let their followers down. Circumstances are such that, as a human being you will compromise, albeit maybe in only a small way, what you have said for what you believe you must now do. You have said that you would always put staff first yet the economic situation is such that the very survival of your business requires you to downsize. Or, less dramatic but no less serious from an integrity point of view, you might have called one of your customers a jackass in front of your staff during a late evening meeting. In the same way as businesses want to define who contributed to the failure of service and how important it is, so too do our leaders. Our default is to pay attention to important issues that we may have caused, as this is where it feels as though our time is better invested.

We forget that erosion of trust comes as often from numerous little things going wrong as it does from the unfortunate big things. But more importantly we forget that our word is not just what we say but also what is heard and understood. So, having worked hard to ensure others see your integrity, it is important to understand how you can retain and regain it when things change. This becomes a lot easier given our definition of integrity as being true to your word. When we realize that we have a chance to put things right, we can do it by following a number of simple steps.

Step 1: admit you have fallen or will fall short of your word

The first thing to do is to admit when we fall short. At the risk of really messing with your head and introducing another song in this chapter, I think we can safely say that in business today, as Elton John would have it, 'sorry seems to be the hardest word.' The key thing to remember is not to justify or state that the failure is the exception. This is the trap I highlight earlier in service recovery. All it does is alienate followers by denigrating the fact that their concerns are justified. Simply acknowledge that you have fallen short on your word.

You may indeed feel that you have not fallen short of your word. You may decide that it is followers who misunderstood your word or didn't appreciate the caveats you put on it. But remember that no one likes the small print. The fact that we shouldn't 'legally' feel we are being let down does not make us suddenly feel happy. You must go back to the first stage of integrity if you fail to understand that your followers' interpretation of your word is how they will judge your integrity. Apply a test of 'reasonable fairness' when it comes to your keeping your word. This is a hard thing to do, especially when your intent was right, but it is necessary if you are to reconnect to your followers.

It is then important for you to articulate how you believe you have fallen short and check that understanding with followers. The best thing to do is state you always endeavoured to do x and you believed that x entailed y and z, but that on this occasion you did a and b. In our examples above you may point to the fact that you always said and genuinely believed that employees came first and that meant you will always look to provide job security yet, on this occasion, you would have to let some people go. By checking at this level of granularity you will not only display an understanding of your followers' concerns but also restate what you are committed to. Of course, apologizing for shortcomings is not enough to recreate a sense of integrity in the mind of your followers. This is why we need our next step.

Step 2: explain how you plan to regain their trust in your word

The next logical step in regaining the trust afforded to us by integrity is to state how we plan to fix things. There are really only two ways in which alignment can be regained. One is by taking necessary actions to realign your word with the situation you are now in. The other is to change your word to fit the situation. The latter is not a facetious point. It may well be that your word was misguided to start with. It may be that the situation was not quite as you saw it. It may also be the case that the consequences of your not having kept your word are such that it can no longer be kept. In any case, changing your word with a clear explanation is a legitimate strategy. Taking our example again you may feel that, actually, with hindsight you should never have said you would put employees first or that you were not clear enough in what you meant (with yourself and others).

Remember, however, that the focus should be on your followers at this stage not on you. So you are not trying to justify your actions but rather to acknowledge their reactions to your actions and explain how your plan to mitigate the problem. The key to success is to restate the connection. What are the steps you are going to take to reconnect to the original word? Is it still valid? Why? How do your latest actions change the original plan?

If you have decided that changing your word is the best course of action, you need to explain why. Be careful that the explanation does not sound like an excuse. To suggest that the situation has changed in ways that you could not expect, and that therefore as a result you had to act against your word, may well be true but it may also suggest that your word is not worth much if it is easily changeable. This is why not trying to justify mistakes is so important. By being able to apologize for a lack of integrity when you should have kept your word, you ensure that a change of word is seen as an exceptional step not a flip-flop for the sake of convenience. Regardless of the strategy you chose, you must now be in a position to reassure followers that you still have the ability to deliver.

Step 3: restate your word and your ability to meet it

It is important to recognize that not having acted in line with your word has had consequences. These consequences must be acknowledged and put right, which is what Step 2 was about. However, whether you propose to renew your promise or change it, it is critical that your followers understand you are capable of meeting the new requirements. This is where we get back to customer service. Earlier on I said that there is nothing worse than the letter that starts with the acknowledgement that we have fallen below our usual high standards of service. This is hollow talk. It means nothing to the person suffering from the consequences. However, once you have apologized and restated a course of action, it is now time to reintroduce your high standards.

The best way to deal with the issue at this stage is to explain how you will deal with the impact of the failure in integrity. By doing so you are both restating your word (either in its original or changed form) and explaining the skills and strengths you have to re-establish alignment. By being open about how you propose to put things right and explaining the strategy you will put in place to monitor the delivery of your word, you put yourself back in the mix of integrity. In effect we started by looking purely at the problem from the followers' point of view (Step 1, apologizing for the consequences of our actions). We then looked at how we can put things right for them (Step 2, restating a course of action). Here at Step 3, we are realigning ourselves to our word.

I am aware that this may all feel like a pretty empty view of integrity. Defining it as alignment seems to narrow the scope to a mechanical delivery devoid of moral consideration. However, in the context of emotional logic, what followers are looking at when they are considering the character dimension is simply your ability to be true to your word. So where asperity provides them with your intent and rhetoric with your articulation of this (your word), integrity becomes the vehicle to ensuring that your words are connected to your actions – nothing more and nothing less. Working on that integration is a critical step to fulfilling the demands of the character dimension.

That being said, there is still one piece missing in the character dimension. That piece is the glue between these disparate elements. It is worth remembering that emotional-logic assessments are not long, rational processes. They are fast assessments made on the basis of emotions and reason. For this reason it is critical to make things as simple as possible. Simple, not simplistic, is key to making the right assessment, so simplicity is what I need to turn to next.

The tweet

Integrity is demonstrating a relentless desire to deliver against your word as well as acknowledging and remedying potential shortfalls.

Note

1   The song 'Jealous guy' was written and recorded by John Lennon in 1971 for his album 'Imagine'. It has been covered over 90 times, most notably by Roxy Music, a band formed by Bryan Ferry in the year Lennon had penned the song. He recorded it in 1981 as a tribute to John Lennon, who died in 1980.

CHAPTER 9
SIMPLICITY

Underpinning question and why it matters

Why is simplicity key to charisma and how can it be harnessed?

Once we have created sufficient emotional resonance to engage potential followers through the values dimension, and equipped ourselves with the asperity, rhetoric and integrity that we need to demonstrate our ability to sustain our vision, there is one key thing left to do under the character dimension. To succeed we must turn our vision of hope into a narrative. That narrative can only be compelling if it meets the requirements of our last element of charisma. That element is simplicity. It is simplicity that provides the impetus for followers to act on our values.

Over the last 10 years or so an important rule has emerged for writers of business books. It is all the more pervasive for the fact that it is unwritten. Let me try to sum it up as best I can for you – Thou shall not write a business book without, at least once, saying something about Apple Inc.

That's the rule. You must tell readers something about Apple. That something has to be either insanely good because, whoever you are, Apple is clearly better than you (that's not a value judgement, simply an economic truth). Or it has to be cleverly irreverent. It can't be bad because you might come across as the sour jealous type. Irreverent though is good. Irreverent makes you look like the cool cat most of us business writers long to be. Truth is, whatever it is you want to say is fine as long as you say something about Apple.

Given this chapter is about simplicity, and simplicity is Apple's domain, this is as good a place as any to obey the rule. There are two things about me that are important for you to know at this stage since they inform the nature of what is to follow.

Firstly I am no rebel. I like to think of myself as a disturbing force and a questioning soul, but as a middle-class parent of two, the closest I can ever come to claiming the label 'rebel' is to make sure the spec of my executive car includes a sub-woofer for me to play what my kids call 'weird French music' slightly louder than is natural for someone my age to do. So by and large, however much I like to think I don't and shouldn't, and some would argue despite my Gallic genes, I tend to follow rules.

Secondly I am an unmitigated Apple fanboy. The late great Steve Jobs then or the amazing Mr Cook now only have to announce that Apple may, in some distant future, produce something unbelievably amazing and I am already down on Regent Street, London, joining the queue outside the Apple Store. I like to use as an excuse that the first computer I ever typed on as a student was a Mac and that as a fast adopter but a slow adapter the whole Windows thing passed me by during the Apple lean years and seems somehow unnecessary now. The truth, however, is far less logical – I am a sucker for the particular type of design Apple provides. Be that as it may, I just love Apple.

However, as much as I find the 'Apple Inc mention rule' difficult to avoid given Apple's association with simplicity, I also find it somewhat disingenuous. No company should ever want to emulate Apple in any way other than economic success. Apple is economically successful because it is Apple. If Apple had tried to be Apple, it would have never become Apple – or something along those lines but you get my point. Copying may be the best form of flattery but it is also a sure road to sub-optimization.

Even if your intention is to learn rather than ape, there is something you have to be very careful of when using anyone as an example, and especially Apple. So much has been written about and so much has been assumed that it is actually hard not to have a distorted view about Apple. Everyone talks about Steve Jobs having a reality distortion field, but actually the most prescient point is not how he distorted reality but rather how little we know of what goes on in Apple. Few others than those who work in the company know the Apple reality and, therefore, we should never take anything at face value, especially when dealing with the complex topic of simplicity.

Simplicity is key to leadership. It is the final step of the character dimension because it helps leaders get through the busy and noisy world followers experience and communicate their character in a way that resonates. It is also a key part of charisma as it acts as a bridge between the character and the achievement dimensions. I will go on to explain its value as well as how leaders can learn to harness it. However, before I do so, it is critical for us to understand what simplicity really is, and that is what Apple can help us do.

On 12 October 2005 the usual anticipation was building. The music was playing. The stage lights were dimming. The scene was set for the most famous turtleneck and jeans-wearing bespectacled man on the planet to appear. And so he did, once again bringing his distortion field with him. For us Apple devotees everything seemed possible when Steve Jobs took to the stage.

That day was no exception; more amazing results were released and beautiful products revealed. But there was one slide in his presentation that stood out. The one slide that, for many in attendance, defined Apple. On it were three remote controls. To the left was a bulky one with the number 48 over it. To the right another bulky one with the number 45 and in the middle, standing proud despite its size, was a small white one eight-and-a-half centimetres high by three centimetres wide (I know because I am measuring mine as I type this chapter) with the number 7 above it.

Steve was making an important point. Here you had it. Here was Apple summed up on one slide. On the left and on the right were what Apple's competitors put you through – bulky remotes with a confusing array of multi-coloured buttons. Apple, on the other hand 'thought different'. Apple thought seven buttons were enough. Not 48, not 45, only seven. In fact, I'll admit it now although I wasn't about to admit it then, I was puzzled the whole time he was presenting. I'm pretty sure everyone involved in the show had worked hard on the slides. Jobs was famous for his attention to details and endless rehearsing of keynotes. However, personally, I had a problem with that slide. I just couldn't see it. I couldn't make out the seven buttons. To me it clearly looked like three buttons (one centred at the top with a 'wheelie' looking one around it and one centred about half way down).

The whole point of that slide was to define 'the Apple way'. Where competitors confuse you, Apple used clever design to make things simple. Simplicity and elegance are not an end in and of themselves. They are the servants of ease of use. Apple makes things simple because they want them to be so intuitive that the product, never mind the technology, disappears and only the experience remains. To you that may be only seven buttons, but to Apple these were its DNA on a slide and those bulky complex remotes defined everybody else.

But hang on. I did make the warning not to take things at face value so let's do a bit of exploring. Who are those competitors? Is Microsoft really full of people who are either too stupid or careless to see the confusion induced by their remotes? Have they become so arrogant that they now have meetings where they sit around thinking about how else they can make our lives more complicated? I'll admit it. I have met some Microsoft people. Some of my best friends are Microsoft people. I find it hard to believe that they 'don't get it'. But hey, Steve had the slide, and he didn't make up the remotes. One of them was the Microsoft Media Centre remote that someone (a committee maybe) had designed. So if Microsoft people are great people, what's going on there? What is it, then, that Apple gets that other people don't? Why do other companies seem so keen on increasing complexity when simplicity is a mechanism that enables us to act? The answer is surprisingly easy – human beings love complexity.

Think about it. Do you really want your remote control to just switch the TV on or off? That wouldn't be a very useful remote control. You want your remote control to have as many functions as possible. In fact you want it to have as many functions as there are 'getting up from the couch occasions'. The more of those functions the less you have to move, which, let's face it, is the whole point of remote controls. As complexity is not the same as confusion, we want each button to have only one function. Given this, it's quite frankly sloppy to have seven buttons. Surely the more buttons, the more functions – and the more functions, the more uses.

In fact, that's exactly the sort of debate Apple gets going after every keynote, and that one was no exception. Not an hour had passed since Steve Jobs had walked off stage before the simplicity versus functionality battle started. It's a fun battle to watch as it is free of casualties, but it is a false battle nevertheless. Yet, as it turns out, understanding the battle lines is key to understanding the importance of simplicity to leadership.

What Steve Jobs had done by highlighting the number of buttons was to equate simplicity with subtraction. Fewer buttons equals more simplicity, he implied.

But given that in most people's minds fewer buttons means fewer functions, doesn't that make the remote sub-optimal? Isn't it just denying us access to the functions we crave? But this idea that simplicity is subtraction is a banana skin Apple unintentionally left lying around for you to slip on. If subtraction was indeed the only facet of simplicity we would always end up with sub-optimal products. Yet, we don't.

In fact, simplicity has another facet that Apple knows but never quite articulates. That's why they have been so successful where so many have failed. They know that simplicity is not just about subtraction; it is also about coherence (Figure 9.1). And it is this notion of coherence that gives rise to charisma.

Whilst we love features, we hate products that don't make any sense. The ones that require us to do a lot of work to understand. The ones that are incoherent. The problem with the Microsoft remote is not that it has too many buttons (it has a lot of functions) but rather that the presence of so many buttons makes it hard to use. What makes the Apple remote a better product is not that it has fewer functions; it is that Apple has made it simpler to find these functions. The key to that simplicity rests in the lone button half-way down called 'menu'.

What Apple did with that one button is dispense with most of the other buttons by transferring the functions to an intuitive, interactive on-screen menu. Whilst our complicated remotes solve our need for features through hardware (one button per function), Apple decided to solve it through software (an intuitive on-screen menu navigated by the minimum number of hardware buttons). That makes the remote simple. What Apple does better than anyone else is work on both facets of simplicity – subtraction and coherence – through the intimate marriage of software and hardware.

It is that definition of simplicity that encompasses both subtraction and coherence that is essential to emotional logic and charisma.

But, 'Apple mention rule' or not, you didn't buy a book about Apple, you bought a leadership book, so what is the point of this dive into simplicity when it comes to leadership generally and emotional logic in particular?

The character dimension sets out a key question prospective followers are asking themselves. The answer will help them make the necessary assumptions

Figure 9.1   Breaking down simplicity

$$\text{SIMPLICITY} = \text{SUBTRACTION} + \text{COHERENCE}$$

against the character dimension of emotional logic. That question is: Does the prospective leader have what it takes to do right by my values and represent my interest? There are two elements to this question. The first element is trust. In order for followers to trust leaders, the leaders need to provide reassurance that they have what it takes ('asperity' and 'integrity') to uphold the vision they project using their 'rhetoric'. The second is the motion element. Followers must understand the nature of the actions required of them. They must be able to picture the demands that will be made on them and anticipate the requirements of followership whilst minimizing the stress they will feel by letting go of their freedom to act for the benefit afforded by being led.

It is simplicity that helps integrate the asperity, rhetoric and integrity dimensions of charisma into the coherent whole required to create momentum. It is simplicity that seals the deal on the character dimension of emotional logic.

Because simplicity is made up of subtraction and coherence, it helps integrate the various elements of the character dimension into a proof point for followers. By showing what they stand for in a simple way, leaders remove the stress associated with giving up some freedom to act in order to step into the unknown realm of followership.

The stress associated with making a followership decision is not caused by uncertainty or complexity; stress is caused by the absence of coherence. The only way to remove stress is therefore to restore coherence. As a customer you do not stress over the fact that your bank is in fact multiple departments, functions and divisions. Stress only occurs when you call the bank helpline to enquire about the balance on your savings account and your mortgage and you are transferred from one department to the next. Or when you change your address and need to fill in a different form for each of the financial products you have, even though they are held by the same institution. At that stage coherence is broken.

To know that banks are complex entities that need to be divided into subsets, helpfully called divisions, in order to work does not alleviate stress. The only way for an organization to remove your stress is to make the organization one coherent whole again. That's what having a personal account manager to handle all the forms for you does. By giving you one single point of contact and accountability, the organization gives itself a face that brings simplicity through both subtraction and coherence.

But what about leaders? What can they do to ensure stress does not preclude you from giving your trust. The short answer is they give you a leadership narrative.

Despite everything others might want to tell you about the need to give followers clarity, it is impossible for a leader to know the future. No one does. But the good news is that, as we have seen with our bank example, clarity is not actually the instrument to use to reduce stress. So leaders don't have to pretend that they know what the future holds. To help followers navigate their lives in the absence of clarity yet without the presence of stress, we need to turn to the concept of narrative environments. Narrative environments are the instruments we can use to build coherence. Narratives are simply frameworks that describe a series of events. I use the term narrative environments to describe the thinking we do when building narratives.

This is an important distinction. Over the last few years, the importance of storytelling and narratives in leadership has been underlined and stressed. That's a good thing. As a result leaders are taught to build visions as stories and narratives. That's not necessarily a good thing.

Narratives only have power if they help followers orientate their behaviours. Stories have been used throughout human evolution as a way of passing on lessons. That can only happen if the narrative carries some familiarity. If you are to relate to the story it must resonate with you. You must be able to picture yourself in it. The danger with just leaders creating stories to sell their vision is that those stories will feel alien to the people receiving them. I often point to the dreaded Q&A documents sent by communications departments in times of change. More often than not these only contain the questions leaders are prepared to answer rather than the genuine, and often awkward, questions of followers. It is because of that necessity for followers to be able to co-create the narrative that I prefer to see the task of leaders as building narrative environments rather than narratives. A narrative environment is designed to engage your followers' imagination, not to just tell them something. In a narrative environment, editorial control is shared.

Narrative environments are the spaces in our minds we use to build those narratives. Studies of early years' development suggest that we make sense of the world through stories. Stories enable us to put a context around what we witness. What is true of early age also holds true in adulthood. We use narratives to interpret and make sense of our environment and the events in our lives. We use narratives to develop our personal and cultural identities and build memories. But we also use narratives to project ourselves in the future. We build narratives to map out our intended trajectory in life (from the work we would like to do to the partners we would like to meet).

Narrative environments help leaders build the simplicity that enables them to pass the character test of the character dimension as well as mobilizing followers to release their discretionary effort.

Stage 1: create a narrative to give coherence

In an uncertain and challenging world, to pretend that we have all the answers is at best dumb and at worst dishonest. But as we saw earlier, it is not answers to the situation that followers seek but rather answers to the question 'Can I count on you to lead me through the uncertainty?' Therefore building a narrative environment requires the prospective leader to prove an understanding of the situation as well as provide a clue as to the road ahead and his/her ability to navigate it.

The narrative environment must contain answers to three key questions:

- Who am I/are we?
- Where are we going?
- Why are we going there?

I purposefully use both the I and we dimensions as the narrative must say something about establishing your role as a leader. It is not so much about your credentials as it is about your values. How you approach situations. The views you hold on the world. It is the glue between the asperity, rhetoric and integrity elements of charisma.

Think back to the Obama campaign of 2008 we looked at in our 'Hope' chapter. Whatever your political affiliation or your views on the 44th President of the United States, the campaign was a textbook example of a narrative that turned a relatively unknown politician into a leadership force. The narrative was built around the story of the unlikely candidate, the community worker who tirelessly worked for the good of people rather than taking on a high-paid job. His views on who we were and where we were going were clearly articulated – 'there is no red states of America or blue states of America but the united states of America,' 'we must be our brother's keeper.' The 'why we were going there' was an appeal to a better America founded on communities supporting each other for the prosperity of all.

Politics is a better place to find narratives as, unlike business leaders, politicians have to appeal to the votes of followers to get elected. But the world of business is not devoid of narratives. The leaders we often describe as visionary are mainly narrative environment builders. By providing a strong narrative that we as followers overlay on business events we imbue them with a sense of vision. Think about Warren Buffett and his annual letter to shareholders or Richard Branson with his daredevil adventures. These build and reinforce narrative environments. One the sage of Omaha who thinks as deeply about the value as well as the values of his investments, the other the fighter for the common man who will disrupt any industry that takes advantage of its customers.

Your role is not to produce a CV as a PowerPoint deck looking at trends and a building strategy. Rather it is to tell a story that helps people build a picture of your approach and your knowledge.

There are three keys that help unlock a narrative – pictures, emotions and situations.

Pictures

Pictures sit at the core of a narrative environment. As we have seen when exploring emotional logic, we think with our senses. It is pictures, sounds, tastes and smells that help us make sense of our world. Pictures are critical because they not only make a narrative clearer but also create an environment for followers to explore.

Think about your vision and your leadership. What pictures come to mind? If you don't see yourself as the artistic type, think about what famous painting summarizes your narrative. What film posters could you use? Putting pictures in the mind of followers enables movement.

Pictures also help to contrast. Remember the importance of contrast we identified with 'asperity'. By painting pictures you offer the chance of differentiation.

Emotions

The aim of any narrative environment should be to evoke emotions. Emotions provide a driving force. We need to remember that in business there are more emotions than just fear. Yet fear is still a preferred default when trying to engage followers. Emotions add granularity and vividness to our thoughts.

The ability of leaders to express their emotions and ignite those of others makes a narrative environment constructive. The best way to make a narrative environment resonate is by picking words that have an emotional resonance and a link to human qualities. For example, to depict an organization as a strong friend who covers our back wherever we are provides a richer (in breadth and emotion) narrative environment than to describe it as a multi-billion dollar market cap global business.

Situations

Finally we turn to situations. Given that we are aiming to bring followers into a narrative environment, offering them specific situations to put themselves in is a useful shortcut to achieving that outcome. 'I was taking a walk in a busy shopping street when I realized the peril of our situation…' To be honest I am not sure what the peril of our situation actually is but I am pretty sure you can picture yourself in a busy shopping street. I am also pretty sure you will have strong feelings associated with that situation. Of course I can't be sure whether these will be feelings of dread or excitement but I know I have tapped a rich vein of associations, as we saw with framing in 'rhetoric' earlier.

The idea is that the more situations you can put your followers in, the richer the environment. And the more you meet the values dimensions criteria and know your followers, the more relevant and resonant the narrative will be. To give them an Excel spreadsheet or a series of bullet points will not create the resonance that a well-targeted story will.

For a narrative environment to be useful, however, it must be portable. That is to say it needs to take on a life of its own, whether or not the leader is present. It must be spread between followers. This is where subtraction comes in.

Stage 2: subtract to get to the core

Just as subtraction on its own does not make simplicity, neither does coherence. To induce followers to take action, leaders must provide a narrative environment short enough to be easily recalled and easily played with by followers. An overly descriptive narrative leaves little room for interpretation, and it is that interpretation that makes followers independent and therefore effective.

As leaders we are versed in the art of subtraction. Business education and economic pressures make us specialists in eradicating duplication. Subtraction is an attractive and comfortable place to start. Yet I have purposefully made it the second step. The reason is that you cannot simplify anything until you know what that something is. It is only when you have all the features organized in a coherent way that you can decide what can be amplified or should be erased or ignored.

You cannot simplify a narrative until you know what that narrative is. The blurb at the back of this book was written after the book was finished. Even if the publisher had a pretty good idea what it might be by the time they had read the book proposal, they needed the narrative before they could extract the summary.

The key to subtraction, however, is to work out what to keep. Like a sculptor removing the excess stone obscuring the final masterpiece, a leader must learn to subtract whilst preserving the core of the goal.

Recently I have been doing some work with senior leaders in a global services business. As part of our work we developed a number of narrative environments that would help followers understand both leaders and visions. One of the participants in that work was called Rocco. Having mapped out a narrative that included both the changes in the environment he and his team were operating under and his personal history, he set to work using the three-box model I shared with you in the 'Hope' chapter. The phrase 'solid as a Rocco' emerged as his answer. Now that might not seem like much. A clever play on words at best. But that little phrase provided a richer narrative environment to his followers than it might appear.

If I tell you that Rocco is the finance director for an organization in the midst of the biggest challenge to its continued relevance and existence since it was founded, 'Solid as a Rocco' takes on a whole new meaning. The narrative environment provides coherence. 'Solid as a Rocco' says that I can rely on my boss to tell it like it is. He will be strong in the face of challenges and do his best to address them. 'Solid as a Rocco' also makes it clear what is expected of me. In our function we don't deviate and we won't bend. We are the rock upon which others can find their way. We assist and support and prop up other functions. It marries both the support and policing roles that finance functions fulfil. It doesn't make any promises about the future that cannot be kept but it answers the fear of change universally experienced by his team with the truth of his character and expertise.

Neither Rocco nor I work for an advertising agency so I am sure a copywriter could do a better job. But 'Solid as a Rocco' is detailed enough to give us a clue as to the narrative yet open enough to make it a narrative environment upon which followers can build. It doesn't matter if Rocco is around when I face an issue, 'Solid as a Rocco' gives coherence to an uncertain world and informs my actions.

Leaders should never pretend to know what the future holds nor should they pretend they can map out the totality of the tasks their followers must fulfil. It may be appealing to hold on to the old adage that the best way to predict the future is to invent. However, a simple moment of reflection on the complex interactive nature of the system we live in will tell you that none of us have the luxury to create the future without having to involve others. What simplicity does is to ensure that followers are attracted to your character by giving them coherence about their role. It is that simplicity born out of subtraction and coherence that enables followers to move from the emotional desire to follow to the physical act of doing so. However the energy of emotional logic can only be maintained if the vision can be delivered. This is where the next dimension of emotional logic, 'the achievement dimension', comes in.

The tweet

Simplicity increases engagement by removing stress. It requires the least number of components (subtraction) working in harmony (coherence).

PART FOUR
THE ACHIEVEMENT DIMENSION

The values dimension offers followers the proof they seek that they are understood, and the character dimension offers the proof that the leader has a vision of the future built on that understanding. But none of this matters without the last element of emotional logic – the achievement dimension.

Whatever leadership model you look at will, at some stage, contain an achievement dimension. The reason is simple. When we look for leaders, we are looking for someone who we trust to do something better than we, alone, think possible. Without a bias for action there can be no leadership.

Followers' emotional logic is attuned to looking for proof points that the potential leader will have the capability to move from vision to action. There are two underpinning questions to which followers seek answers. The first is: 'Can the potential leader translate words to actions?' The second is: 'Can they take those actions?' These are the two final elements of emotional logic and of charisma – measurement and action.

The achievement dimension of emotional logic

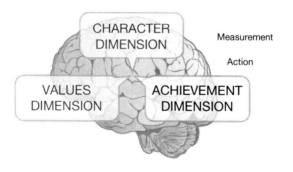

CHAPTER 10
MEASUREMENT

Underpinning question and why it matters

Why is measurement critical to leadership and how is this revealed?

To meet the requirements of the achievement dimension of emotional logic, leaders must rely on their ability to demonstrate progress, or at least their ability to progress, towards the vision they outlined. Progress can only be determined if markers are in place. Measurements are those markers. They give depth to charisma as they give followers the ability to differentiate between leaders who deliver promises and those who show the promise to deliver. To be useful these must resonate with followers. The best way to achieve resonance is through the co-creation of those measures.

The British started it but it took the French to name it (possibly highlighting deep cultural traits in both nations – the British do whilst the French talk)! Historians are still debating today whether French diplomat and envoy to the new United States of America Louis-Guillaume Otto's 1799 description of the world being in the midst of an 'industrial revolution' is indeed an appropriate description. The truth is that by all accounts the process of change was more gradual than the sharp correction in trajectory implied by the term revolution. Yet no one argues that the period ranging from the mid-18th to the mid-19th century changed our world.

It was Great Britain that spearheaded the changes. Machines reinvented work. Starting with the textile industry, the relentless march of progress had a profound impact on economic and social structures. Mass migration from the countryside led to ever larger cities. Canals, railways and roads, necessary for trade, changed a rural landscape into an industrial one. Population and incomes grew as never before. This first industrial revolution accelerated even further and became known as the second industrial revolution with the arrival of steam, internal combustion and electrical power generation.

Every generation likes to think that change is happening at a pace never before experienced. We all describe our world as a turbulent one. Yet, it takes very little imagination to see how, as the agricultural age was turned upside down, our 19th-century forbears would have seen the arrival of steam engine as disruptive in the way that we experienced the later introduction of the search engine. It is at that time that two remarkable men entered the world. And it is important that these two remarkable men must now enter our story.

Successfully navigating the requirements of the achievement dimension of emotional logic is entirely dependent on our ability to set measures. Measurement is the only way followers can assess progress towards a vision, and your ability to make progress towards a vision is what is at play here. Measurement matters and the two men you are about to meet can teach us something about measurement that few others could.

William Thomson and Gustave Bonickhausen may not be names you are familiar with, but they have left indelible marks on our world. Both were born in the early 19th century (1824 and 1832 respectively) and their lives seem to be mirror images of each other. Yet these lives somehow intertwined without the two ever meeting.

Born in Glasgow, Scotland, to a teacher and engineer at the Royal Academical Institution, William, despite serious heart problems that would see him almost die at the age of nine, proved himself a precocious and academically minded young man, entering Glasgow University at the age of 10 (not an altogether unusual feat as it was common for talented students to do so at a similarly early age).

Born in the town of Dijon, France, from German immigrants, the young Gustave, on the other hand, never seemed destined for academic greatness.

As he found school boring and a waste of time, his tutors at the Lycee Royal didn't hold much hope for his future.

Both discovered an early interest in literature, but whilst a young Gustave was being pushed by his teachers to study more seriously, William at age 12 was already winning prizes and praise for his work (translating at this time Samosata's *Dialogues of the Gods* from Latin to English). Not content with this achievement, the young William went on to publish a number of well-received scientific essays under the pseudonym PQR.

At a time when the idea of different types of intelligence had not yet been raised, William and Gustave provided stark examples of the different ways in which individuals can succeed. As is often the case with childhood education, mentors and tutors had a major impact on both their professional paths. William was encouraged to pursue his interest in academia and science whilst Gustave's uncles tried to develop in him an interest in vocational learning and engineering.

The one similarity between the two youths was their parents' unwavering support. Although they never actually met, the boys' paths would eventually cross in Paris. William was sent by his parents to study French, Gustave to prepare for his entrance exams to the impressive Ecole Polytechnique. William succeeded whilst Gustave, as was his habit with education, failed.

The mirroring of their two lives did not stop there. An exemplary mind, William was proving an exceptional mathematician. As Gustave's mind was turning to the engineering feats of Britain, William's was drawn to the mathematical work of France. He turned his efforts to another Frenchman's theories, at the time when the British establishment, still enthralled by those of Newton, was rejecting them. Sadi Carnot's theories on heat and heat engines were being rejected by the famous heat scientist James Prescott Joule. Joule was failing to discredit Carnot so Thomson took it upon himself to investigate. And if we ever needed more connections between Gustave and William, you may be interested to know that Sadi Carnot came from a long line of engineers, scientists and statesmen whose surname would eventually be given to the school Gustave had attended as a young man in Dijon.

William's academic career continued its incredible rise in Cambridge. Upon seeing his work, one of his Cambridge examiners told another, 'You and I are just about fit enough to mend his pens.' At age 22, after having been made a Fellow of Peterhouse in Cambridge (a college he had only entered a few years earlier due to his father's generous support), William took on the chair of natural philosophy at his beloved Glasgow's university. The precocious student had donned the professorial robe at his alma mater a mere 12 years after first crossing its threshold.

Gustave on the other hand entered the more vocational Ecole Centrale des Arts et Manufactures in Paris, where he developed an interest in chemistry. Upon graduating, he did not get the job he craved at his uncle's Dijon vinegar factory. Instead he began his professional life under the tutelage of the railway engineer Charles Nepveu. A number of jobs and companies gave him the opportunity to become a fully fledged railway engineer, building bridges and stations across France.

Both men travelled extensively. Gustave went to Egypt were he looked after the building of locomotives for the government, then built infrastructure throughout Europe and invested in the building of the Suez canal as well as undertaking contracts for the 1867 and 1878 World Fairs (Exposition Univer-selle) he had first visited as a young man in 1855. William's travels saw him criss-cross the Atlantic at the head of a number of expeditions to lay trans-atlantic cables on the sea bed. A keen yachtsman, he travelled to Brazil and Lisbon to oversee a number of cable projects.

True renaissance men, William and Gustave were always attracted to adjacent fields to those they professionally mastered and had views on most things. Of course even the brightest can be wrong and so it was with William, who in 1896 famously declared in a letter declining an invitation to join the Aeronautical Society: 'I have not the smallest molecule of faith in aerial navigation other than ballooning, or of expectations of good results from any of the trials we hear of.' He went further in 1902 where he was recorded to have said in an interview: 'No balloon and no aeroplane will ever be practically successful.' Should he have added the word 'profitably' somewhere in the sentence then his prediction could well have been right, but as it was he missed the rise of aeronautics. Gustave, in contrast, became enthralled by the subject.

Having witnessed the power of air movement on the buildings he had built as an engineer, Gustave was keen to explore the possibilities of aeronautics. As much as William was a scientist who became an engineer, Gustave was an engineer turned scientist who had a critical impact on the development of aviation. In 1913, he was awarded the Samuel P Langley medal by the Smithsonian Institute. Alexander Graham Bell, who presented him with the medal, commended him for his work on air resistance in connection with aviation.

Whilst you may indeed not recall the names Bonickhausen and Thomson, Gustave and William are no strangers to your world. In 1892, aged 68, William Thomson was ennobled for his work and politics. As is traditional upon being given a title, he changed his name. In honour of his roots and his work, he chose the name of the river that flowed near his Glasgow laboratory as his title. William Thomson became Baron Kelvin of Largs, known to us as Lord Kelvin. It is that name that was given to the unit of measurement of absolute temperature that he devised and we all learn about at school.

As for Gustave Bonickhausen, the Frenchman of German descent, he too changed his name. In his case it was not ennoblement that made him, aged 48, change it. Rather, it was only in 1880 that he officially decided to formally adopt the names his parents had taken upon coming to France and by which he had always been known. Gustave Bonickhausen thus became Gustave Eiffel. As William had done, Gustave adopted a name from a natural landmark. His surname derived from the Eiffel mountains of his parents' native Germany – mountains that, at their highest, are just over twice the height of the tower that forever bears Gustave's name, and over eight times the height of New York's Statue of Liberty, the metallic structure of which he engineered.

The history of both men is interesting in itself. The lives of great inventors, scientists and entrepreneurs always make for fascinating reading. But it is not their lives nor indeed their work that is of interest here, but rather their philosophy and legacy.

I promised you both men could help us with the measurement concept, and indeed both had an innate understanding of the power and necessity of measurement as the determinant of knowledge and progress. Their work was driven by a need to understand. They both realized that understanding is born of measurement. Together, they were part of the measurement revolution. It is that revolution that is so critical to the achievement dimension of emotional logic.

As we enter the last part of our journey through charisma we are faced with one of the remaining questions of emotional logic – 'Will this person be able to bring the hope they embody to pass?' That leaders have a resonant vision (the result of the values dimension) and that they will uphold the values necessary to bring it about (the result of the character dimension) are necessary, but are not sufficient conditions for followership.

We are surrounded (mainly through self-selection and choice) by people who share our values and have sufficient character to do right by those values. The achievement dimension goes one step further. The achievement dimension deals with the assumptions followers make around some key questions. 'Can I be sure, that, should I trade my self-determination for the security of their leadership, they will be able to make hope a reality?' 'Do they have what it takes to deliver on the promise of their character?' One thing is for certain: followers will never have the answers to these questions unless there are some ways to show progress is being made. Only measurements can reassure and there are no better masters of measurement than William and Gustave.

We all know of leaders who created resonance with their vision and enthralled us with their character. We have all voted for politicians who believed what we believed and promised what we desired. We have done these things only to be disappointed when these leaders seemed to forget what they stood for. We have all experienced the let-down of the promises turning into losses and retractions. But how often did we stop to ask: 'Did they deviate from the road or was the road so badly signposted that we forgot we were on it?' Did the leaders spend so much time painting a bright picture of the future that they forgot to paint the clouds along the road? Did we forget the brightness that was to come when the sky got obstructed by the first temporary cloud, or were we duped all along? Did we get it wrong when we assessed integrity or did the leader simply lack measurement?

It was at the age of only nine that a young William wrote a few telling lines from the Alexander Pope 1734 poem 'Essay on Man' on the title page of one of his essays entitled 'On the Figure of the Earth'.[1] The lines were an early warning of a lifetime obsession:

> Go, wondrous creature! mount where Science guides;
> Go measure earth, weigh air, and state the tides.

From Cambridge to Glasgow via Oxford, from mathematics to engineering via physics, from William Thomson to Lord Kelvin via PQR, he never stopped measuring.

As noted earlier, if the journey Lord Kelvin travelled was one from scientist to engineer, Gustave Eiffel's went the opposite way. Having built a successful career as an engineer, he devoted the rest of his life to science and, in particular, the science of measurement. Having retired from his Compagnie des Etablissements Eiffel, he made his way up his tower. Every day he climbed the winding thin metallic stairs to his top-floor office. Once there he would engross himself in the measurement of aerodynamic forces that had for so long impacted his work on ever-larger structures. He developed new instruments of measurement. He stretched a cable from the second level of the tower to the bottom so he could spend hours dropping objects down the cable to measure their resistance. His legacy is full of novel ways to measure. We owe wind tunnels to him for example.

Both men knew that measurements are the currency of progress. Both understood that whatever determines our trajectory through history, it is measurement that helps us understand our progress. It is indeed the case – as Eiffel once predicted when he said 'I ought to be jealous of the tower. She is more famous than I am' – that it is the structures he left behind that are associated with his name, but we would do well to remember that it is his ferocious appetite for measurement that has left them for us to see. Human progress can only exist if it can be measured. And so it is for a leader's success.

Whilst the first sentence of one of Lord Kelvin's famous quotes is a prescient reminder that guessing the future is a dangerous game, the second sentence of that quote best sums up the place we find ourselves in as we come to the achievement dimension of emotional logic:

> There is nothing new to be discovered in physics now. All that remains is more and more precise measurement.

Those measurements didn't only impact the field of thermodynamics in the case of Kelvin or aeronautics in the case of Eiffel. They also left an indelible mark on the world of business. There is a quote from Lord Kelvin that many business leaders use but seldom attribute, never mind acknowledge. In its original form it reads:

When you can measure what you are speaking about, and express it in numbers, you know something about it; but when you cannot measure it, when you cannot express it in numbers, your knowledge is of a meagre and unsatisfactory kind: it may be the beginning of knowledge, but you have scarcely, in your thoughts, advanced to the stages of science whatever the matter may be.[2]

The reason it is seldom attributed is that, as is often the case when business borrows from science, the quote has since become a lot more pithy, but its meaning a lot less clear! Bastardized and forever diminished by the business community, Kelvin's famous observation on the interplay between measures and progress became the hackneyed and ad nauseam quoted 'what gets measured gets done.' But 'what gets measured gets done' doesn't only diminish the value of Lord Kelvin's words, it also exposes leaders to catastrophic consequences. What gets measured gets done is wrong. What gets measured gets done is poor logic (after all only what has been done can be measured). What gets measured gets done is a flawed belief.

By leaving out the fundamental truth of Kelvin's statement, the power of the quote has been lost. There are a number of steps between measurement and action that need to be identified. To be closer to the truth 'what gets measured gets done' should in fact read as follows:

What leaders are interested in, they measure. What gets a leader's attention tends to get a follower's focus. What gets attention and focus gets talked about. What gets talked about is seen as important. What is seen as important gets done.

I grant you that's not a sentence you are likely to quote in your next meeting but it identifies the three factors at play when trying to meet the requirements of the achievement dimension and underscore the importance of measurement. These are:

- *The need for clarity*
  We only know what we can measure. Any form of progress necessitates measurement. A vision is a form of progress. When we look to our leaders' values and character, we look to gauge both their current view of the world and their future vision for it. This vision only becomes clear when it can be measured. Becoming a leader is about being able to quantify a vision so as to make it real, rather than just qualify it to make it desirable.

As Lord Kelvin noted, 'only when you can express it in numbers do you know something about it.' Measurements are necessary to bring clarity to the vision. That clarity enables followers to make an emotionally logical choice.

- *The need for standards*
  When followers ask 'will they be able to deliver?' they are looking for a yardstick to measure achievements against. Without this signposting they cannot hold the leader accountable for progress. Without this accountability, leadership fails.

  What makes leaders poor, in the mind of followers, is their failure to reassure us through thick and thin that they are following a course towards the realization of their vision. Measures offer the standards against which we can gauge leadership effectiveness. What standards will we uphold when judging whether a leader is upholding our values or not? How will we know?

  By offering measurements towards fulfilment of the vision, leaders give reassurance that they are prepared to be held to account. When the road gets tough followers will look to those standards to judge leadership effectiveness rather than judge the effectiveness of one course of action over another. Any deviations on the road only become issues if standards haven't been clarified in advance through measurement. As Lord Kelvin said 'without measurement your knowledge is of a meagre and unsatisfactory kind.'

- *The need for credibility*
  For any measure to be a successful marker of progress it needs to be credible in the minds of followers. If they do not recognize the measure as being a proper indication of the progress of a mission, it will not fulfil the conditions of the achievement dimension. By rejecting the measure followers will reject the leader.

I am reminded of my early days in consulting when colleagues and I would try to decide how successful we were in achieving our aims. The measures offered by our leaders were common to most consultancies – utilization (paid consulting days), sales (financial size of contracts) and quality (feedback from clients). Whilst these make perfect business sense, they tell you little about your respective worth as a professional (too many success factors are beyond an individual's control). So we preferred one other key measure – air miles.

Our belief was that the more air miles you had, the further your name resonated outside the UK. If a client was prepared to fly you, you must have been a great consultant. You may or may not decide that we had a point (our leadership certainly didn't and air miles were seldom talked about in end-of-year performance reviews). The point, however, is that our measure was what we used to determine our success. Our leaders' measures, and as a consequence they themselves, were largely ignored.

The way to make measures credible is to co-create them with followers. This is not only best practice when dealing with a piece of work to be done, it is critical when dealing with leadership itself.

If co-creation is critical when dealing with measurement, then we have a problem. I refer to that problem as 'the Elvis fallacy' and I have argued a number of times in a number of places that this Elvis fallacy is one of the biggest corporate mistakes of all times. I call it the Elvis fallacy after the song 'a little less conversation, a little more action please'. The fallacy is attractive as we all have a visceral reaction to words like meetings and collaboration. We know these things will slow us down and, in the current climate, speed is important. Yet we need to remember that the very essence of measurement is that what gets talked about gets done. What gets discussed gets achieved. The fact that our conversations have been less than perfect does not negate the need for them.

So given that the need for measurement is critical and that the measures that will successfully meet a follower's requirements need to be created through conversations, how do we go about conducting conversations that are generative yet efficient (for the want of a better word)?

I first met David Cooperrider when we shared a speaking platform at a conference in the Netherlands. Professor of Organizational Behaviour at The Weatherhead School of Management at Case Western Reserve University, David has that unassuming yet powerful presence the best academics tend to have. Watching him speak with his soft engaging tone, it is no surprise that he has managed to facilitate the conversations of some of the most influential business people in the world. Having an ego strong enough to cope with yet mature enough to appeal to big egos is a difficult balance for most to achieve. He does achieve it and what is more he achieves it with aplomb.

In 2004 he was asked by then United Nations Secretary General Kofi Annan to facilitate the coming together of 500 business leaders in an unprecedented summit on global corporate citizenship. To facilitate the conversation in a way that would lead to action, David used his technique of appreciative inquiry[3] – a way to look at the world from a position of strength rather than weaknesses.[4] In our words here, he used a way to generate a common vision that could be measured and enacted. It is that technique that I want to introduce here for the purpose of bringing clarity, standards and credibility to the achievement dimension. David identified four steps to making a vision concrete enough to be enacted.

Stage 1: discover

Most business education tends to be done through a deficiency lens. We come to leadership assuming there are existing problems to be solved. We analyze organizations to identify problems and develop strategies to fix them. This mindset automatically puts the leader–follower relationship as one of superior–inferior. Followers have a problem they have been unable to fix and the leader can rescue them.

The dynamics of charisma however are different. Charisma relies on a relationship of follower–leader, not one of victim–rescuer. The key to meeting the requirements of the achievement dimension is to build a feeling of trust among followers that the leader has the potential to fulfil a vision rather than to correct a course. The emphasis is therefore not on deficiencies, but rather on successes. Rather than asking 'What do we need to do to get there?', the process starts with the question: 'How do we know we can get there?' This is what the discovery stage of appreciative enquiry is about.

The purpose of this stage is to uncover the strengths and successes that underpin the hope the leader offers. This stage invites followers to look back at past successes. Having presented a vision of where we want to be, the leader stages a conversation about followers' previous experiences of being there, forcing an inquiry into what went well rather than what is broken. Followership requires hope to encourage, rather than fear to coerce.

The discovery stage builds confidence in followers that the road ahead can be travelled whilst also fostering the social bonds necessary to build cohesion around the leader's vision. Even though our reliance on technology to drive our social interactions tends to hide the fact, conversations and connections are fundamentally different. By starting our enquiry into measurement with conversations around successes, we encourage the kind of enquiry Lord Kelvin was referring to when he postulated that 'to measure is to know.' Conversations ensure a shared understanding and a richness of stories and experiences are revealed.

In practice you should get your followers to talk about times they have witnessed peak performance around them. Those times when vision was being achieved. For example, if your vision is one of a highly collaborative workplace, ask followers to discuss times at which they sensed they were operating in a high-collaboration environment. The role of the leader is to encourage followers to find those moments and share them with others. Politicians are adept at using rhetoric to take followers back to better times. 'Remember when…' may well take many different forms but often lies at the core of political speeches. In business this may not be used as often but the generative properties of 'When was the last time you experienced us doing this well?' are the same.

By identifying, discussing and sharing the factors that led to a successful achievement, followers not only point to the elements that will mark progress along the road to achieving a vision but start to build confidence that the achievement of the leader's vision is not only possible but probable, given past experience. This confidence is key to passing the achievement dimension test.

Stage 2: dream

The next stage of appreciative inquiry is one David calls dream. Dreaming is another one of those words that doesn't seem to fit so well in the corporate dictionary, even if it is the first word to come up in the entrepreneurship one. Rather than the dream we saw in our chapter on hope, or the one so perfectly used by the master of rhetoric who was Reverend Martin Luther King, this dream is focused on merging the vision of the leader with the stories participants have revealed at the discovery stage. This is the stage that will ensure the Elvis fallacy isn't committed.

Followers are encouraged to look at what the organization/community could be. Of course most business leaders are used to this kind of visioning. The main difference is small but it is critical. Unlike a visioning exercise that is designed to elicit a road to avoid or get over problems, this exercise forces the participants to look at the organization on the basis of its strengths.

In many ways it is more narrow than a general brainstorming on the art of the possible, but, like the scientific experiments Kelvin and Eiffel conducted, the discussion focuses on observable and measurable strengths emanating from the discovery stage. These discussions will build credibility for the vision, given that the future is revealed as a direct result of existing realities. These conversations generate a series of positive statements on where the organization wants to be (ie a practical application of the vision that reinforces the joint followers–leader values).

If we take our example of a collaborative workplace you may, for example, end up with statements like 'we trust each other to deliver...' Whatever the statements are, you can see how they start to identify tangible (ie measurable) elements of the vision that will bring clarity and standards as times get tough, which they invariably will.

Stage 3: design

This next step is when we get into measurement. This is about translating the discussions of the discover and the dream stages into the road map that underpins the success measures. The discussions are used to work out how our statements of intent can be put into practice. Steps are taken to ensure the fulfilment of the intent. It is these steps that give rise to the measurements that indicate progress for followers.

In our example above, we may decide that 'We trust each other to deliver' will be translated into a number of steps such as: 'We will set up clear goals for everyone and report weekly on progress'; 'Reports will be shared amongst all individuals involved in the delivery of the goal.' These measures not only keep everyone focused on what needs to be done but they put down the markers necessary to ensure we see progress being made. This will ensure the sustainability of leadership.

The examples I have chosen are of course short range and somewhat pedestrian. Clarity is easier to give when the issue is small. We can, however, imagine how these conversations can be generated with a larger constituency and a broader goal. If we go right back to our chapter on hope and the Obama campaign's focus on 'reclaiming the American dream', it is easy to see how this would need to be translated into a number of key measures before anyone could agree progress had been made.

The role of the leader is not necessarily, in such a case, to manage conversations personally. An aspiring presidential candidate may deliver stump speeches to a crowd rather than sit down at every dinner table in the country. In such cases the leader manages the conversation by encouraging followers to recall stories of success (discover), to which a series of steps can be attached. A politician might therefore describe 'reclaiming the American dream' in terms that highlight each step:

- Step 1: 'Remember when we used to look after our neighbours.' This encourages the recall of particular stories at the discover stage.
- Step 2: 'We will rebuild the communities that we have lost.' This is the positive statement of the dream stage.
- Step 3: 'This will require us to review the way we look at taxes in my first term' (insert increase or decrease depending on your political affiliations). This identifies the measurements required at the design stage.

Without this process the leader is likely to set targets and incentives that are either disconnected from the followers' narrative (ie misaligned to the values and characters a follower had identified) or unclear to the follower (ie not appropriate as measures that show progress towards the achievement of the mission).

Stage 4: destiny

The last step David encourages in his methodology is the destiny stage. This is when the actions are taken to deliver on the vision. In the methodology, this step is highlighted to ensure that everyone is involved in making things happen. For our purpose, it reinforces the role of leaders as facilitators of narratives that followers own. It is a good reminder that leadership, unlike role-imposed leadership, is dependent on followers giving power to the leader. Leaders must clearly articulate how the measurements translate into individual actions.

Of course, the leader will still have a role to play in the enactment of the vision. In fact, the elements of the character dimension are geared towards making sure the leader will be able to live the hope they embody. The destiny step is therefore, in itself, a critical piece. It helps us move from measurement to action. As such, it deserves and gets special attention in followers' decision-making process. This is why I have decided to devote the last chapter to this idea of action.

So, as we come to the end of this journey through charisma we should have potential followers who are drawn towards leaders on the basis of their values and character and who are reassured that the road ahead has been mapped and can be achieved. All of this, however, will be of no use unless they also believe that those leaders have a bias for action. We want to know that the leaders we invest our trust in have the capability to act on the basis of the promises they make. This bias for action is the final determinant of an emotional-logic decision, and that is where we will go next.

The tweet

Measurements ensure followers can track progress. To be effective they must be clear and credible, which is best achieved through co-creation.

Notes

1 *An Essay on Man: Moral essays and satires*, Alexander Pope, Cassell & Co, 1891.

2 *Popular Lectures and Addresses*, Vol I (1889) 'Electrical units of measurement', delivered 3 May 1883.

3 I must also thank my good friends at Public Service Management Wales for their incredible work in disseminating information of value to leaders. In particular Dr Neil Wooding, the Director of PSMW, for passing on to me a great booklet he wrote in collaboration with Roger Rowett on working with Appreciative Inquiry. If you happen to work in the Welsh public sector (sorry to everyone else!) get hold of the AI edition of *Sowing Seeds*. Well worth a read.

4 For more details of David's powerful approach you can read any one of the numerous books he has written. I recommend *Appreciative Inquiry: A positive revolution in change* by David L Cooperrider and Diana Whitney (Berrett-Koehler, November 2005).

CHAPTER 11
ACTION

Underpinning question and why it matters

Why are actions critical to emotional logic in general and the achievement dimension in particular?

Actions are the litmus test of charisma. They are critical to followers both at the decision stage ('Will the potential leader have the ability to act?') and during the act of following ('Is the leader acting in line with my values?'). Actions determine how much and for how long a leader will be followed. They are the final stage of charisma but also a way for followers to link back to the values dimension of emotional logic for a continual assessment of a leader's performance.

If Malcolm Gladwell is to be believed and we choose our leaders on the basis of height[1] then, standing at an average-busting 6ft 5in, Vittorio Colao was always going to become a leader. And so he did when, as a young conscript in the Italian military, he became a reserve officer in the elite military police force, the Carabinieri. Although Vittorio himself would later highlight his service in the military as an important influence on his life and leadership, what is of interest here is his current role as CEO of one of the world's largest mobile telecommunication companies, the global telecoms giant Vodafone.

Having worked alongside Vittorio and his team for some time, I have witnessed the climate of engagement he engenders in the company along with the praises he receives from shareholders and the thanks he gets from beneficiaries of the Vodafone foundation. I can therefore vouch that there are many qualities and achievements other than his height that make him deserving of the role. But there is one in particular I want to focus on.

Vittorio Colao is a master communicator and storyteller. From a walk in the slums of India to a first communion gift, via British Airways' new first-class cabin refit, there is not a single experience Vittorio cannot turn into a business lesson taught through a story. His ability to construct an argument (rhetoric) and bring others into the discussion (simplicity) make him a formidable inter-locutor. There again, given a career that has straddled the worlds of consult-ing, publishing and communication, you would expect him to find the 'mots justes'.

Of course, it would be as silly to postulate that communication skills alone enable you to become the CEO of a major corporation as it is to suggest that only height does. As a McKinsey alumnus, Vittorio doesn't shy away from numbers and analysis. His global career path as well as his natural enthusiasm also ensure that he has forgotten more than I'll ever know about the sector he operates in (and the man seldom forgets anything). The granularity of his knowledge is a case study in asperity. Having had the chance to work with many executives and CEOs, I would suggest that one thing that differentiates him from others is this ability to simplify by marrying the conceptual and the analytical and then to translate them in a way that others can engage with.

Whilst it may be strange to start a chapter devoted to actions with an example of great communication, especially given the old adage that actions speak louder than words, there is method to my madness. One thing I have heard Vittorio say repeatedly is: 'a poorly communicated innovation is an innovation that does not exist in the eye of the customer.' It is for that sentence that it was important to me to introduce Vittorio to you. The sentence appeals to me for three reasons.

The first is that it is true in that obvious, common-sense way we often forget. I have witnessed so many projects where the time spent on building an elegant and excellent product or service is wasted as the results go unnoticed by customers. Communication is often an afterthought, something we hand over to the marketing department at the end of our efforts. Vittorio is right: no product or service, however great, has an innate right to exist. It is cus-tomers who give it that right. It is communication that gives them the impetus to do so.

The second reason I like the phrase is that it takes me back to my under-graduate years spent puzzling over philosophical problems. One that attracted me in particular was the problem first postulated by philosopher George Berkeley in 1710 and taken up by William Fossett some 20 years later. I am sure you have heard the problem, which is typically expressed as something along the lines of: 'If a tree falls in a forest and no one is there to witness it, does it make a sound?' There are many ways to understand the problem and answer the question. Personally I have always liked *Scientific American*'s 1884 answer. 'Sound is vibration, transmitted to our senses through the mechanism of the ear, and recognized as sound only at our nerve centres. The falling of the tree or any other disturbance will produce vibration of the air. If there be no ears to hear, there will be no sound.'[2] It may be a scientific rather than philosophical answer but nevertheless it is an elegant one!

The third reason why 'a poorly communicated innovation is an innovation that does not exist in the eye of the customer' is a sentence with which I wanted to start this chapter is because what is true of innovation and customers is true of leadership and followers. As leaders, we may well spend a lot of time deciding which actions to take but unless these are witnessed by our follow-ers, unless there are eyes to witness them and ears to hear them, our actions do not exist. And that is critical to the achievement dimension.

Measurements give a roadmap to a leader's intent but it is actions that give reassurance that the journey is progressing. This is why actions are so critical to charisma. They provide proof that progress can be made, and sustain leadership by showing it is being made. Of course, we are talking here about followers deciding to follow a leader, so the actions they can rely on for assurance they are making the right choice are either historical (the leader's track record) or aspirational (their stated intent). That's when Vittorio's rule of communication comes in. To build assurance, we must ensure that both our historical and aspirational actions resonate in the right way. Like our tree falling in the forest, if no one is there to witness our actions, we must ensure they are communicated.

Here is the problem though. Leaders make hundreds of decisions and take countless actions every day, often resulting in followers receiving hundreds of messages everyday (not to mention the thousands of messages they receive in the ordinary course of living their lives: advertising, news etc). In my book *Leadershift* I called this 'the attention trend'. As people we are bombarded with more information and messages than our attention can cope with. As followers, the only way to cope is through some form of filtering. Not a blog post, tweet or tech conference goes by without the phenomenon of 'curation' (choosing, editing and maintaining our information) jumping out of the relative historical shadows it inhabits to claim its place in the spotlight. In many cases this act of curation is achieved by narrowing our circle of trust (we listen first to our Facebook friends, we only read the same newspaper or feed every day...). To have any chance of being followed, a leader must be included in that circle of trust. As I always say in my speeches, what chance have you got to be followed if people don't even know you're there?

Of course, in our organizations, it is often clear who the leaders are. Or rather it is clear who the titled leaders are. In fact leaders are watched carefully by followers for cues on what is important and how to behave. We saw in our chapter on integrity how critical the alignment between thoughts, words and deeds is, for the very reason that leaders are closely observed. Any disso-nance will be immediately spotted. However, the fact that leaders are closely watched is also an asset. It means that they do not have to change much before it is noticed by all. This fact alone gives reassurance to many leaders that most of what they say or do is heard and witnessed. This, however, does not take away from the importance of being aware of the attention trend. The fact that their voice is heard does not, in and of itself, mean that they are clear or understood.

A leader cannot afford to communicate everything. This would only add to the ambient noise and would not make the choice any clearer for a follower. Rather we have to determine which actions matter enough to be communi-cated. This is where the leader becomes a curator.

Interestingly, both 'curator' and 'manager' contain the same idea. In museums, the curator's role is typically to decide which objects should be collected as well as overseeing the cataloguing and care of the objects. In that sense, lead-ers are curators of their own actions, deciding which ones should be taken and communicated.

And just as larger museums have multiple curators caring for different collections, leaders must understand that their actions fall into a number of collections each requiring different emphasis and communication. Under-standing these different collections is Stage 1 of building a coherent action strategy to answer the emotional logic needs of followers. Having identified the different types of actions available to them, leaders must plan an impact strategy (Step 2) as well as a relevant communication strategy to ensure these resonate (Step 3).

Stage 1: clarifying the action collections

There are two kinds of actions – two wings to our museum if you like – which split into further categories – our museum collections (Figure 11.1).

Figure 11.1   Hierarchy of actions

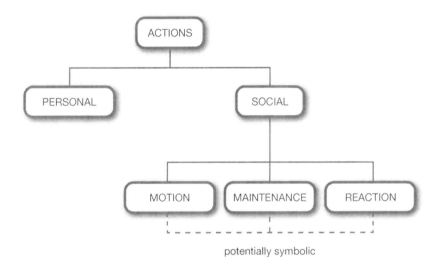

potentially symbolic

The two main kinds are personal and social. Personal actions are normally described as the behaviours a person displays and are based on their desires and beliefs. If I desire to be rich and believe the best way to do so is to rob a bank, then I can take the action of robbing a bank. It is my desires and my belief in the way these can be satisfied that lead me to take a particular action or set of actions. This is a very rational view of actions, and we know from Part I that rationality is not always a determinant of our actions. There are countless examples of people undertaking actions because they believe they must, even when they have no innate desire for the outcome. The key here is the agent-centred nature of the action. The action is driven by the agent's desires with no regard to the social context, other than in so far as it impacts these desires.

Leadership actions on the other hand are a different kind of action. Leadership actions are not personal actions. With leadership actions the social context is key to achieving the desired outcome. Leaders vary and change their actions depending on the social context. It is their followers' desires and beliefs that will decide the outcome of the leader's action. Social actions have meaning beyond the personal desire of the leader as they engender actions on the part of followers.

Of course, a leader's personal actions matter. They are a good way to spot integrity, which is critical to fulfilling the character dimension of emotional logic (but we have gone over that ground before). However, it is important at this juncture that we focus our inquiry on social actions. It is social actions that will help meet the demands of the achievement dimension.

There are three main categories of social actions that are worthy of our focus, as their presence will determine potential followers' ability to fulfil the emotional logic achievement criteria.

Motion actions

Motion actions are actions that are part of achieving a plan. These actions are designed to move the plan forward. They are planned and form part of a strategy for the achievement of an objective. I may decide that to achieve the vision for my business I will need to invest in a new plant, recruit and develop new staff, or go to the money markets for funding. These actions may well sub-divide into other, smaller actions but overall they all form part of my motion actions.

Maintenance actions and reactions

Maintenance actions and reactions on the other hand are those that are taken in the normal course of events. They are the everyday actions that are necessary to fulfil a plan but are not necessarily designed to move it forward. Like reactions, which are forced upon us by events, maintenance actions are not ones that have been planned for but they are necessary nevertheless.

Of course you would hope that in the course of business all maintenance actions and reactions reinforce motion actions; however, the distinction is useful as they will require a different kind of communication. When maintenance actions are mistaken for motion actions, followers quickly get the notion that little progress is being made. It is only by communicating the distinction and the links between the two clearly that followers can possibly have the right perception of the leader's intent.

Symbolic actions

Symbolic actions are not different from maintenance or motion actions per se. What is different is the way they are taken. For example imagine having to fire a dishonest member of staff for gross misconduct. That's an action. It is either a maintenance action taken in the course of the normal business of performance management, or a motion action taken, for example, to address the shortcomings of an underperforming unit of the business. What makes it a symbolic action are the repercussions it has for people not directly connected to the action.

There is one famous story that went around a few years ago, when Jack Welch still headed GE, that he once called two of his most successful sales people at a conference and sacked them for displaying the wrong behaviours. He was making the point that whilst they achieved results they went about it the wrong way.

I have heard this story recounted numerous times in numerous settings. I am not even sure it ever happened. In fact, I once consulted with an ex-GE senior leader in a financial services firm who was fond of saying that while he worked at GE he sometimes wished he had worked for the company he kept on reading about.

That is the point of symbolic actions. They take on a life of their own. Whether they are myths or legends, they become stories people tell.

There is one facet of the GE story that is not helpful as it reinforces a stereotypical view of symbolic actions: namely, that symbolic actions are big actions. That is not the case. Yes, putting a man on the moon and bringing him safely back to earth was a symbolic action. But removing the partition wall between the executive dining room and the workers' canteen, as one of my clients did, is also a symbolic action. And so is passing on an invitation you have received to an event to a member of your staff you feel deserves it. The value of symbolic actions is entirely dependent on the reaction on the part of the witness or recipient of that action, not their size.

Let me add a note of caution about symbolic actions however. They must be used sparingly. Firstly, because their value lies in the element of 'surprise' they offer. By their very nature they must stand out as being outside the norm. Secondly, because symbolic actions can distract from the everyday, real and at times banal set of actions required for actual progress to be made towards the achievement of the stated goal.

Of course it would be disingenuous of me to ask you to maintain a detailed agenda of the kinds of actions you conduct each day. You are far too busy acting for that! I also know that whilst your capacity to think is high, it takes time to reflect – and I have been advocating far too much reflection throughout this book to believe that you still have room for more. However, I would suggest a simple high-level audit – a kind of gut feeling if you will. In percentage terms, what kinds of actions occupy your time? Can you easily identify the symbolic actions you have taken? Action-awareness is to action-management what self-awareness is to self-management – a necessary starting point. But a starting point is all it is.

Moving to the management of actions, necessary if we are to have the impact we need, requires asking a different set of questions, demands asking different questions. When you identified the symbolic actions you took, were they symbolic because you intended them to be so or did they become so in the minds of your followers despite your intentions? Do your actions always have the impact you desire? Do you ever take the time to think though the social impact of your actions, even when having to react quickly? How far down the organization do you think about the impact if you are a senior leader?

Stage 2: planning an impact strategy

To know which actions to focus on in order to ignite the emotional logic of others requires focusing on the impact that is necessary to attract the right followers. In the context of the achievement dimension, where followers are looking for reassurance that the vision can be enacted, it is the social actions that matter. We need the right followers to respond to the right actions, and to achieve this these need to be communicated in the right way. Don't worry; as I mentioned earlier, I am not dismissing personal actions but their impact is covered by the integrity element of the character dimension.

Interestingly, in our quest for followers, we seldom stop to consider the type of followers we want beyond skills and attitude defined through role descriptions. We develop profiles and segments that we pass on to recruitment agencies or HR departments. Yet, we know that what we really want is more granular than that. Most of us have an image, even if grainy or blurred, of the person we are looking for. Of course, we may need to be challenged. We may need to have our horizons broadened. But whatever the outcome of discussions, our picture might alter, yet it is still a richer picture than the words on the job specification.

Picture in your head a man. The man is in his sixties. He has a title, and has properties in London as well as a large country estate. Over the last 40 years or so his romantic life has been the subject of endless speculation and countless news reports. He is divorced with children.

Who are you picturing in your mind? My guess is that you are more likely to have someone resembling His Royal Highness the Prince of Wales, Prince Charles, rather than Sir Mick Jagger of the Rolling Stones. The point is that the above description covers both adequately and imperfectly in the same way – same description but widely different personas. And persona rather than demographics matters when planning an impact strategy.

To target our impact we must understand behavioural patterns, motivations and attitudes alongside the more common demographics on which we normally focus.

The way to develop these detailed portraits is to start with the simple and move progressively to the more detailed and complex information. Whilst taking account of such criteria as age and gender is forbidden in many countries when it comes to recruitment for work, education, socio-economic class and experience might be useful basic information to start with. They will help you develop a mental model of the followers you need. However, these basic data points alone will not help you determine a plan for your impact.

To fully understand how to best appeal to the emotional logic of potential followers through the achievement dimension, we must develop a narrative of their lives. Where do they shop? Where do they get their news from? What do they wear and why? What are their life goals, their dreams, their expectations?

This may all sound rather esoteric and far removed from our concern here, but these are the things that differentiate Prince Charles from a rock legend. The more colour you can add to your personas, the more it will help you target the communication of the actions that matter. Of course, you may inject the persona you are trying to create with insights gained at the values dimension stage of emotional logic. The dimensions of emotional logic are intertwined not separate. The achievement dimension is about the reassurance potential followers seek that you will be able to bring the hope to reality.

However, this is not about researching particular people but rather about defining a persona for those we hope will rally behind our leadership. Compassion helps you understand the concerns of potential followers, whereas developing a persona will help you understand the practicalities of meeting these concerns.

I remember a discussion I had with a CEO in the car-parts industry. Whilst his job was in the automotive sector, he personally did not care very much what kind of car he drove, until one of his branch managers pointed out the disappointment of his staff that the company CEO did not seem to possess a car commensurate with the image they had of a successful boss of a successful company. He wanted to get from A to B whilst they wanted to see an inspirational image of what they could become. You may well feel, as both he and I did, that a big executive car could have separated him from his staff and even engendered resentment. Whilst his compassion made him understand that they wanted a leader who understood their need for an image of success, it was an understanding of their persona that told him the actions required to bring that compassion to life. A persona helps us understand how we can best weave our own leadership narrative with that of others.

Having developed a rich portrait of potential followers, the next stage in developing impact is to determine the kind of actions that will impact them. Let's take the example of our leader above. What the manager was telling the CEO was that his followers demanded some symbolic action that would demonstrate his understanding of their aspirations.

So let's suppose that our CEO bought a new, large, tinted-windowed luxury saloon with a chauffeur to boot. Would that have done the trick? Are the jet-flying, executive-car-driving, Manhattan-apartment-living CEOs only tolerating their luxury lifestyles to make their staff more secure in the knowledge that their boss understands their aspirations? Not quite! Again, remember the model is not linear. Compassion will help followers gauge your intent. Integrity will help them gauge how much that intent is linked to your actions. Measurements will help them gauge whether progress is actually being made. But one other thing that will help them gauge your achievements is the rounded nature of your actions. Symbolic actions alone do not bring the reassurance you can deliver the hope.

The key to success is to determine the right combination of maintenance, motion and symbolic actions to take for the persona you need. There are a series of questions that will help you determine the shape of that combination. In the measurement chapter we looked at what milestones mattered – are the motion actions clearly aligned to these? What would the follower persona classify as a motion action versus a maintenance one? Looking at the balance of actions I have taken over the last week or month, how would followers have ranked these?

Making an in-depth assessment may not be necessary, but developing an innate understanding of how your potential followers will view your actions is. The hope that you projected will only be of value if potential followers think you can deliver through your actions. If the balance of your actions mainly tilts towards the maintenance type, or is perceived as such, followers will not naturally put you in a leadership position, however great the outcomes.

But of course no amount of segmentation and profiling will ever guarantee genuine communication. Many segmentation exercises fail because the science takes over from the humanity. The exercise becomes sterile. As the focus on action is about igniting emotional logic, the way we communicate actions becomes paramount. As we saw before when considering rhetoric, integrity and measurement, dialogue is a two-way stream with involvement on both sides through narratives. The last critical stage is therefore to determine and enact the right form of communication.

Stage 3: executing the right communication

I was careful when recounting Vittorio Collao's words to say 'an innovation that is poorly communicated' rather than 'an innovation that is not communicated'. The word poorly matters a lot to actions. The key is not to communicate but to communicate in the way that has most impact on the decision-making process of followers.

There are two reasons we need to focus on communicating actions well. The first, which I mentioned earlier, is the extent of the demands already made on our potential followers' attention. If we cannot break through the noise, our actions will go unnoticed. Communicating actions is not enough; we need to communicate them in such a way that they will be noticed. The second is the nature of followers' reactions. There is a direct causal effect between the way an action is perceived and the reaction we allocate to it. You will recall the *Guardian* advert I mentioned in the rhetoric chapter – the one with the skinhead running towards the briefcase. Our perceptions dictate our responses. A leader's scope for direct impact is limited, because our impact is filtered through followers' frames.

Imagine you are the CEO of a global burger chain. Data tells you that customers have to wait too long for service. Taking the action of going down to your nearest restaurant and flipping some burgers yourself is unlikely to have a major impact on reducing global lines. Doing it with a camera crew and some photographers and showing it on your in-house TV, however, might be the symbolic action you need to gather your troops. But then again it may be perceived as a gimmick that has the exact opposite effect to the one you intended. So how do you make the call, if indeed a call needs to be made?

Symbolic actions tend to polarize; hence the need to make sure you have the right follower persona in mind when taking them. As we saw with asperity, polarization is not a bad thing if it is driven by what you stand for. Trying to appeal to everyone equally will leave you with an average rather than great followership. But whilst actions without communication might be invisible, actions without thoughtful communication do not guarantee the desired reactions.

There are four important elements to a communication strategy: your goal, the audience, your message and the tactics. Understanding the types of actions and the followers' persona will help you meet the requirements of these elements to form a plan on how you communicate. My aim here is not to help you devise a communication strategy in the same way your internal or external communications departments might help you do.

This is not about a formal approach to building a plan but rather a planned approach to a thoughtful action strategy. From the moment I mentioned building a brand in the hope chapter via the chapter on rhetoric, I have made the point that leaders are communicators. That is different from communications professionals. The aim is for you to develop the sensitivities needed to make sure the right things come across, as opposed to developing the expertise necessary to do things right. The latter can be bought in, but the former is priceless. So with that caveat in mind let me take you through the different elements.

Goal

Of course each action you take, regardless of whether it is a motion or maintenance action, will have a goal. For emotional logic the goal of the action is the impact it will have on your potential followers. For each of the actions you take, the primary question to have in mind is therefore: 'What do I want my followers to think, feel, say and do?'

Now in the case of a politician standing for election, the actions will be past ones that will be a proof that this person has what it takes to follow through on promises. If elected, the actions will serve as proof that followers are right to continue giving their trust and support. In the case of past actions, the answer to the question 'What do I want them to think, feel, say and do?' will help you narrow down the types of past actions you have taken and select the most appropriate to put forward.

Audience

The audience is either the people you know you want as followers, or the persona you have designed of who they ought to be. You may have a sophisticated segmentation with primary and secondary targets. In fact, the more senior you are or the more complex the environment you operate in, the more likely this is to be the case. In a complex organization involving multiple

stakeholders, how your audience will in turn impact theirs is a key consideration. In that case you might need to develop multiple personas. To prevent
these multiple personas from making your message schizophrenic, you must
target your message to your primary audience (what you want them to think
and feel) in a way that will impact their own audience (what you want them to
say and do).

Message

The message should be driven by the vision you are trying to achieve. It links
the action you have taken or are taking to the hope you are trying to convey.
It helps followers be clear on the issue you are trying to address, the problem
you are trying to solve or the effect you are trying to have. As we saw in the
rhetoric chapter, facts do not speak for themselves and nor do actions.

Of course in the work of a busy day many actions will be taken, but to have
impact communication should be sparse. By clarifying the message you are
aiming to deliver, you will be able to bundle together groups of actions that
speak to the same message and communicate these as one. In the example
of President Obama I used earlier, to communicate that he was a community
organizer (his CV) and that he helped mobilize communities to generate hope
(the actions), he does not need to go through each and every one of the small
actions he took. He only needs a proof point for that message to resonate.

Tactics

Finally, we come to the element that will make or break your communication,
and for which it has been so important to understand the types of actions
leaders take and the personas of a leader's potential followers. Tactics are
the whos and the hows that will help your message stick.

There are many ways in which you can communicate, and as we saw earlier
with our burger chain CEO the same message, delivered in the same way,
can yield dramatically different outcomes depending on the audience. Having
understood the personas, you need to reflect on the tactics that will bring
about the best result.

Is the communication a simple utterance of the actions taken, or should it
take the form of a symbolic action? What symbolic action is most relevant to

your audience? What media should you use? Trust is based on intimacy, so whilst written communication can be powerful, a call may be better. Recently, when working with a group of executives selected by their leaders as high potential, we decided to communicate some of the work that they had done not as a presentation or a meeting, but instead by distributing a newspaper in tabloid format with a number of articles in it. The portability of the medium, as well as the surprise of finding a newspaper rather than a PowerPoint deck, helped the message circulate and generated more trust in the message. Remember that communication and the way we make decisions are not just rational things – instead the whole body plays a part. The tactile nature of the medium matters.

The point of communication is to ensure that your credibility shines through each and every action you take and thereby reinforces the achievement dimension of emotional logic. In a crowded, noisy world, you will need to be creative to reach your audience with impact. That creativity may also mean that less communication that is better targeted will give the sense of quiet confidence your followers need. There is no such thing as too much communication; there is, however, too much bad communication.

Before I close this chapter, let me reiterate that whilst actions are the final point of our tour around that most mysterious of words that is charisma, which I hope I have managed to demystify for you, they are also a link back to the beginning of our inquiry rather than merely the end. The way you complete the achievement dimension will have a direct reinforcing or mitigating impact on the way followers continue to perceive you under the values dimension. The cycle is never ending and self-reinforcing as long as the follower–leader relationship is in place. It is this symbiotic relationship between the dimensions that dictates that the development and maintenance of charisma must be continuous.

So here we are. First I must thank you for making it this far. I buy about five business books a week and finish only a few. Whilst our publishers take hope from this, as authors that fact alone haunts us. So if you are reading these lines, and on the assumption you didn't just turn to the last page to find out 'who dunnit', I owe you a debt of gratitude. But, please, if I may have a bit more of your time I would like to offer a couple of reflections by way of closing thoughts on what may help you sustain your progression through the stages of emotional logic.

The tweet

A poorly communicated action is an action that never happened in the eyes of your followers.

Notes

1 Gladwell, M (2005) *Blink: The power of thinking without thinking*, Allen Lane.

2 *Scientific American*, 5 April 1884, p 218.

CONCLUDING THOUGHTS

A map, however detailed, does not make a navigator.

I am all too painfully aware in my consulting practice that having great leadership models does not guarantee great leadership development practices, never mind great leaders. By way of closing I would therefore like to offer you some reflections and principles on how to undertake a development journey. As the title suggests these are only thoughts. They are neither restrictive nor prescriptive.

Research suggests that the people who buy good parenting books are not bad parents looking to improve but parents who are already good looking to better themselves. It is not good parenting books that make you good parents but the fact that you are bothered enough to buy them, which indicates that you are likely to be good parents looking to improve.[1] In fact, Steven Levitt, the economist of 'Freakonomics' fame, argues that it is who parents are rather than what they do that makes a real difference. The fact that they are buying parenting books only goes to show that they are the kind of high-achieving parents with the health, intelligence, lifestyle and economic status that makes them more likely to be good parents. Correlations do not guarantee causalities.

I believe the same is true of leadership books. My assumption is that the people who read these books are either looking for affirmation that their practices are sound or for ideas they could use to improve, or indeed both. Given this, I am clear that you already have your own practices, which I have no wish to replace. My aim is not to patronize you but rather to outline some of the practices I have witnessed that I have found, over time, make a difference to the sustainability of a development journey.

But before I offer you the principles I have come to rely on, I must outline the concerns that have driven me to articulate them as a way to help the people who have been kind enough to seek my guidance. So let's start with the two concerns that may derail any efforts to develop.

As Levitt suggests, who you are matters as much as what you do. Yet, I do worry that our practice of leadership development takes place to the detriment of character and personality. We are at our most effective when we are ourselves. However, when unchecked, the proliferation of leadership competency models, to-do lists and habits lists may well lead to the development of an homogeneous mass of clones: leaders who are neither adept nor adaptable. Remember the ideas in the asperity chapter? Many people I have discussed these with either worry that I am advocating bullying or are relieved to hear that the impatience and demanding behaviours they have been told to tone down are actually acceptable. Of course neither position is quite valid with respect to what I advocate, but that the debate still rages is testament to the fact that we are worried about being ourselves.

We are paralysed by the deluge of information about what constitutes healthy, productive behaviour. We are so reluctant to stand out that we run the risk of not standing for anything. Yet, as we saw in the introduction to this book, the behaviours and competencies we are told to practise are not necessarily aligned with the behaviours we observe in the leaders we admire, nor are they the behaviours others value in the leaders they seek.

Which brings me to the second worry I have about our development practices. It is the worry that led me to write this book. We are stuck in a mindset that makes the leader the most important variable in leadership.

Given that in most organizations it is leaders who nominate other leaders rather than the followers who choose them, this is an easy mistake to make. However, as I pointed out early on in Part I, even if followers cannot elect their leader, they will vote with their discretionary effort on how successful the appointed leader will be. Our need for leaders existed before our industrial model and will live beyond it, but in the meantime, our education system, professional or otherwise, is stuck in a mindset unrelated to the needs of our times. We are developing leaders on the basis of the needs of our organizations rather than those of our followers.

Of course the real picture is not as dark as this. Much work is being done in both the social and professional sphere to address some of these shortcomings.

There are many educators, development professionals, consultants and practitioners who are seeking to redress the balance by creating experiences and avenues that take personality and followers as their starting points. I have also been lucky to meet a lot of aspiring as well as established leaders who are successfully developing and practising 'follower-resonant' leadership. So, as promised, let me offer you some thoughts on the development practices I hope will help you navigate the map this book provides. There are four principles that will help you retain your authenticity as you continue to meet the demands of your followers.

Principle 1: there's a tick in 'authentick'

The first principle is a rather straightforward one to explain, yet much harder to stick to.

I have always been appalled by trite business sayings like 'There's no I in team' (there should be) and 'Assume makes an ass of you and me' (it doesn't). Yet I also will admit to being fascinated by their staying power. The ultimate test of this is not only that we remember them but that we seem so keen on spreading them. So for the last decade, in search of fame, I have been trying to come up with my own.

So here we are. There's a tick, in 'authentick'. It may not be a copywriter's dream nor will it probably be on every businessperson's lips any time soon but that's the best I could do and in any case I like it. The point is simple – the starting point of any leadership development effort, and especially the charisma development that I advocate in this book, is entirely dependent on authenticity. The very premise of the book is that you will always sub-optimize your impact if you try to be someone other than yourself. And you cannot be authentic if you don't understand what makes you tick. To be yourself you have to know yourself and what you stand for.

To help you maintain this supreme principle, there is another critical development principle that over the years I have come to talk about when helping executives at every level of organizations think through their personal development. This is principle number two.

Principle 2: surround but don't surrender

People are always keen on giving advice. Everyone has a view, an opinion, a pet model or a pet hate that they like to share. Even if you are high up in an organization and the people below you find it hard to give you feedback, peers, analysts and shareholders won't be shy about dispensing their views.

While surrounding yourself with advisers enlarges your view, you should not surrender to their advice. It is your leadership, your principles, your points of view that will activate emotional logic. Becoming a mouthpiece for the conflicting views of others or acting purely as a curator or integrator of those views is a sure way to fail in engaging others. This is the hardest balancing act of leadership. It is the ability to learn the reality from people who find it difficult to voice it whilst isolating yourself from the noise that people with vested interests make.

That doesn't, of course, mean that you should be stubborn and unwavering when faced with a reality that questions the very essence of your views. Unfortunately, reality is a much more fluid concept than what we would like to believe.

They say the Queen of England thinks the country smells of fresh paint because everywhere she goes people have just repainted the buildings. Followers are keen for leaders to get the best view of a business, even if that view distorts reality. To remedy this kings and queens throughout history were keen on having jesters who could keep them grounded by telling them how things really were.

Kings and queens have also been surrounded by advisors and nobles, all with vested interests and all seeking a particular outcome. The same is true of leaders today. Remaining grounded, breathing the air outside the executive bubble we mentioned in Part I, is difficult.

My little boy is keen on the rather tasteless (pun intended) joke of the polar explorer who upon asking local people for advice is told to remember never to eat the yellow snow. Yet, I am amazed at how many people still do.

Of course, there is inevitably a need sometimes to do things you don't enjoy. You may have to spend a lot of time reconciling differing viewpoints or making calls that are not easy. But you should never compromise and end up doing something you know is wrong. Reconciliation is necessary but compromise never is.[2]

When you find yourself hesitating before taking a step, ask yourself whether the hesitation is because of the pain this necessary step will cause or it is due to the fact that this step is the wrong one. Hesitation is a good indication that something you are about to do needs thinking through. I am not talking here about the big ethical choices, which should be easy to make, but rather the everyday dilemmas for which there is no real 'right' choice. There is nothing that is more important than preserving your integrity, and integrity is more often lost through small compromises than by big wrong choices. Being courageous and steadfast will ensure that the emotions you arouse in others last.

To be advised and influenced without being hijacked, the best leaders I know have what I call a strong philosophy of work. I recognize that, as you would expect from a consultant, the term 'philosophy of work' sounds somewhat pretentious and nebulous. The best leaders develop a personal view of how visions are developed and businesses grown. They have their way and approach that they can share and use.

Our walk through charisma contains the building blocks of this approach and whilst the content may change as the problems and opportunities evolve, having a personal approach will ensure you remain true to what you believe. The next principle on my list should help you do this.

Principle 3: think Madonna and child

Biology, pharmacology and technology are combining to enhance our cognitive abilities. Professor Kevin Warwick of the University of Reading developed an implant he and his wife carry that directly links their nervous systems. The quest for telepathic communication, omitting the need for mechanical speech, is viewed as the next frontier.

I am all for progress but at the same time can't help wondering how unintelligible we would become if we had direct access to what was going on in other people's brains, never mind how unnerving it would be to know what others actually think. The reason it would be hard to make sense of what we would discover is that our mechanical voice is in fact multiple neurological ones. That is not to say we have multiple personalities but rather that our personality is composed of numerous self-talks all going on at once.

It is this multi-layered self-talk that helps us regulate our behaviour. Going back to the introduction to these thoughts I need to point out that what I fear is not self-regulation of behaviour. Rather, what I am afraid of are the consequences of suppressing rather than regulating our drives and instincts. We are human precisely because we are able to self-regulate by channelling these towards the actions that the moral and cognitive 'we' want to take.

I have developed a simple test for self-regulation that I call the Madonna and child principle. It simply states that if your mother (the Madonna) would be ashamed of whatever you are considering doing, or if you can't explain it to a six-year-old (the child), or both, then don't do it.

Effective leadership relies on you having a strong moral compass and being aligned to this moral compass and perception of others (the Madonna test) and the clarity of your intent (the child test). The Madonna and child test preserves your integrity and, in tandem with my next and last principle, should enable you to make the most critical of development decisions and choices.

That last principle is of rather more tactical nature. It is designed to ensure that it is possible for you to work practically with the first three.

Principle 4: buy an egg timer

Time is the biggest development tool. I am not talking about time as in 'It takes time to develop' but time as in 'You need to take your time to think things through.'

To develop as a leader you need to understand who you are as this underpins all the dimensions of emotional logic. To understand who you are, you need to reflect. Whilst you can think quickly, reflection takes time. I am not advocating a retreat or a long reflective walk, although I would if I thought you might do it. But realistically, I know few people can drop everything to go for a walk. What I am advocating instead is developing an ability to think things through in the moment. If you can't think things through in the moment you will end up doing it at home or at night, neither of which is fair on the ones you share your home and your nights with.

So buy an egg timer and put it on your desk. Don't try to get away with a watch or a guess – there is something powerful in the novelty and physicality of the egg timer. It also helps you signal in a playful way to others around you that you are thinking and value this thinking time. When faced with a decision to make, turn over the egg timer.

Of course you will be the judge of what decisions deserve the 'egg timer' treatment. But please don't make those so big that you never use the technique. Do not allow disruptions or discussions.

There you have it: the four principles that should become your satellite navigation system as you travel the road of personal development.

I realize my chosen career is a strange one. As a conference speaker I know that there are few other occasions in life where you will be given the opportunity to speak uninterrupted for an hour. As an author I also know that people seldom give you uninterrupted hours of their time to try to absorb your thoughts. What makes this career even stranger is that I chose this very one-sided world in order to generate multiple-sided conversations. My sincerest hope is that you will discuss, critique and criticize the ideas this book contain with those around you, and if ever you feel the need to include me in those conversations feel free to contact me. Thank you once again for having given me your time.

Notes

1　The economist's guide to parenting; full transcript available on http://www.freakonomics.com.

2　For an in-depth look at the difference between reconciliation and compromise I would urge you to turn to the work of someone I admire and am lucky enough to count as a friend, Mr Fons Trompenaars, and his work on culture and dilemmas.

INDEX

3

CPSIA information can be obtained at www.ICGtesting.com
Printed in the USA
BVOW030036200313

315968BV00001B/1/P